The *BIG* *Picture*

INTEGRATING CHILDREN'S LEARNING

Edited by Keith Pigdon and Marilyn Woolley

ELEANOR CURTAIN
PUBLISHING

Dominie
$24.95

First published in 1992
Reprinted 1995
ELEANOR CURTAIN PUBLISHING
906 Malvern Road
Armadale VIC Australia 3143

National Library of Australia
Cataloguing-in-publication data :

Pigdon, Keith
The big picture: integrating children's learning.
ISBN 1 875327 14 2.

1.Interdisciplinary approach in education.
1. Woolley, Marilyn. II Title.
372.19

Production by Sylvana Scannapiego, Island Graphics
Edited by Ruth Siems
Designed by Sarn Potter
Cover design by David Constable
Cover photograph by Keith Pigdon
Photographs by Keith Pigdon, Paul Molyneux, Kath Murdoch
Typeset by Optima Typesetting & Design, Melbourne
Printed and bound in Australia

CONTENTS

PREFACE

This book is an outcome of the collective efforts of a great many teachers who have worked together in a sustained way to improve their practice. The work centres around the subject Curriculum Integration, which was introduced into our Primary Course at Melbourne State College in 1979 as a means of addressing the fragmentation of the curriculum in our schools. Over the years, many practising teachers have responded constructively to our intentions and shaped the model we advance in the book in ways which are suited to their context, beliefs and practice. Their responses have influenced our work considerably and we warmly acknowledge their various contributions.

In addition to the chapter contributors, several other members of the Department of Curriculum, Teaching and Learning at The University of Melbourne have had a significant impact on this work. In particular we wish to thank Geoff Poynter, a gifted educational leader who has contributed in innumerable ways, and Jean Mitchell who was involved with us for a very productive three years.

Finally, we thank our fellow writers who have shared responsibility for the book and given generously of their time and resources in its production. The book remains an artefact of the continued sharing and interaction between the teaching team.

Keith Pigdon
Marilyn Woolley

INTRODUCTION

Effective teaching and learning enables students to grasp some of the 'big ideas' about the world which they need to know. These ideas are concerned with the nature of complex phenomena in our world — living things, the environment, lifestyles and institutions, the ways in which technology has changed our lives and the natural environment, and the issues associated with these changes. Some approaches to teaching these ideas are fragmented and simplistic and make it difficult for students to develop an overview or 'big picture' of how their world works. These fragmented approaches have also made it difficult for teachers to develop a 'big picture' of curriculum.

This book brings together teachers' practice and students' learning within a framework of integrated curriculum. Its aim is to help teachers make informed curriculum decisions which lead to the establishment of a learning environment where students are encouraged to confront and consider important ideas and decide the most effective means of communicating these ideas to others.

Our approach attempts to maintain a balance between structured teacher planning and interactive learning. It involves teachers in being explicit about what they want the students to learn and how they want this learning to occur. This means that teachers will have clear purposes for the selection of appropriate resources, activities, grouping strategies, record-keeping and student assessment procedures.

The chapters present a model for planning and implementing integrated curriculum units, a case study of a particular unit on the environment, a discussion of the role of language in integrated learning and an exploration of student assessment and evaluation within this framework. The book concludes with a consideration of the issues of implementation at a classroom and school level.

The Big Picture provides an overview of what is meant by integrated learning and places it within a framework allowing readers to adapt and modify the information and suggestions to their own circumstances. Examples of successful classroom practice are used extensively throughout the book along with suggested activities for teachers to implement in their own classrooms. Over the years, the authors have been actively involved in classrooms and this book serves to acknowledge the achievements of the students and teachers with whom they have worked. We hope that this work will help you to define, or refine, your own 'big picture' of integrated learning.

1
THE CONTEXT
AND THE
FRAMEWORK

Keith Pigdon and **Marilyn Woolley** articulate a framework of ideas and approaches to integrated learning which they have been advocating for over a decade. They argue that the essence of 'big picture learning' lies in the ideas which drive teachers' curriculum planning and provide the purposes behind the teaching and learning strategies.

◆

INTRODUCTION

This book addresses the escalation of demands on teachers and the consequences of this for student learning. It suggests an integrated approach as a constructive response. Every day, teachers are faced with the problem of what to do and what to leave out. There are increasing feelings of guilt about the implications of these daily decisions and the frustrations which flow from trying to balance what has been done with what might have been done. Some weekly programs have come to resemble television guides. The time slots are filled out so that what is to be done at a given time on a given day is recorded, but there is no obvious connection between the events. In many ways, this reflects the pressures generated by specialist teachers, special events such as Book Week, sports afternoons, and the need for access to particular facilities such as computer equipment. These may well be worthwhile and legitimate activities, but they cut across the sustained activities and approaches which are the essence of the systematic development of knowledge, attitudes, values and skills in our schools.

Unintentionally, many teachers have instigated a 'stop-start' curriculum. This is how it might look to a student in a Year 2 classroom:

9.00 Class singing of 'The Fox' and 'I'd like to Teach the World to Sing'
9.05 News — four students share recounts of where they went and what they did on the weekend. One introduces news of an earthquake in Chile.

9.15 Handwriting patterns using the letter 'y'

9.30 Mathematics — automatic response to tables, simple addition and subtraction. Consolidation of place value to 1000

10.30 Morning recess

10.45 Spelling — 'Have a Go' cards. Rhyming words from *In the Garden of Bad Things*

11.05 Language workshop — silent reading of free choice books. Responding to reading activities. Conference on *Pippi Longstocking*

11.45 Health — the five food groups. Planning a well-balanced breakfast. Conducting a survey of weekly breakfast patterns

12.15 Lunch

And so this fragmentation continues across a given day, within a given week.

ESTABLISHING THE BIG PICTURE

There are no real connections between what a student might be doing in any of these time slots. Many of the tasks remain incomplete, often leaving learners frustrated or alienated. Even if completed, they remain atomised, fragmented tasks which might help to develop skills in isolation, but are unlikely to contribute to the development of 'big picture' learning which helps the learner make connections and gain a sense of control or ownership.

How many people practised the piano for many years, developed quite a sound technique and a repertoire of skills, but one day closed the lid of the piano and never touched it again? This response can perhaps be explained in terms of the fragmentation of isolated tasks, the inability of the learner to imagine how these tasks are connected with the kind of competence they are pursuing, and the failure to experience the joy which accompanies big picture learning and knowledge. It is the experience of **connectedness** which matters. The lack of connection means that learners undertake tasks in a confused and meaningless fashion. This is confirmed by a powerful study of literacy by Wickert (1989) who pointed out that one in three Australians can read but are unable to 'get the point' or make connections.

A SENSE OF PURPOSE

A student's life at school is a critical time. For them, ten (or more) years of attending school may seem an eternity. Within a lifetime, it forms a small but significant part. Above all, it is compulsory. Anything that *has* to be done should have a clear purpose to those undertaking it:

A child's school day should make sense. It should be about something. Ideally the various activities of the day should work together, building upon one another for some purpose. (Simpson 1990, p. 26)

Students' predictions about what they will be doing in the year 2000.

Many students do not experience the cohesion which is implied in this statement. For them a day at school is more like a tabloid sports. They move from activity to activity without any broad sense of purpose, other than the completion of the task, and with little control over their learning. They are aware that winners are emerging but the prizes remain something of an illusion.

For some teachers, a school day can seem like an obstacle course. They struggle to get through a multitude of tasks, but time is against them and they worry about the many things they can't complete. Teachers, too, need a clear sense of purpose:

> *A teacher's day should also make sense. Teachers who can see a wholeness and simplicity in their curriculum have an easier task of organising their day than those who are frustrated or intimidated by what they interpret as the increasing complexity of the curriculum demanded of them. (Simpson 1990, pp. 26-7)*

THE CROWDED CURRICULUM

The past three decades have brought vast changes to the way in which schools operate and to the nature of the curriculum. Pressure from a wide variety of sources has led to the inclusion of many 'new' subjects or curriculum components such as media studies, technology studies, gender studies, personal development, multicultural studies and peace education to name but a few. Even within those subject areas that have been with us for a considerable time there are new pressures, such as the demands of achieving basic literacy competence in a modern technological society. Though these developments have been worthy inclusions, they have, in a collective sense, created problems for or increased pressure on teachers.

Meanwhile, teachers are expected to continue with everything they have done in the past and somehow find time to include the 'new' areas. Imperatives to include new areas are rarely accompanied by a list of other things which are no longer necessary!

We need to consider the essential elements of the curriculum and look at how we can develop a program that achieves connections between the disparate and competing slots of time. In other words, how can student learning be made more effective in the time we have them at school, and how can our planning, organisation and evaluation become more efficient and meaningful? This book proposes that this can be achieved through an integrated approach to teaching and learning.

AN INTEGRATED APPROACH TO TEACHING AND LEARNING

An integrated approach allows learners to explore, gather, process, refine and present information about topics they want to investigate without the constraints imposed by traditional subject barriers.

Once learners become engaged in exploring and expressing ideas, their learning is relevant and purposeful. In these learning situations, the ideas (content) and the ways they are processed (sorted out) become inextricably linked. Our model of integration plans for this to happen systematically and makes a distinction between subjects containing the big ideas about how the world works and subjects which allow learners to process these ideas. The model provides a framework for planning and organising topics

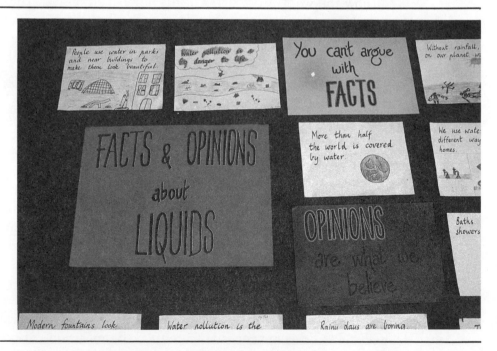

Students' analyse the differences between fact and opinion.

containing ideas about how we live, how we work, the influence of technology and media on our lives, the market system, the natural and built environment, energy and force, the nature of matter, space and time, life cycles, what it means to be healthy, and personal relationships. These topics are drawn from subjects which we classify as the **content subjects.** They include social education, media studies, multicultural studies, science, technology studies, environmental education and personal development.

In developing their ideas and understandings about the way the world works, learners use a variety of means (visual, mathematical, linguistic, performance) to explore, organise and represent their understandings. We classify these as **process subjects.** They include language, art, mathematics, music, movement and drama.

CONTENT SUBJECTS	PROCESS SUBJECTS
Social education	Language
Science	Art
Environmental education	Drama
Personal development	Mathematics
Technology studies	Music and movement

Figure 1.1: Content subjects and process subjects

In essence, integrating the curriculum involves the integration of content and process. The **content** subjects are essentially concerned with ideas about how the world works. The **process** subjects offer a range of ways of allowing us to represent how we see and make meaning of our world (real or imagined).

Michael Halliday's model of the ways in which language is used can help us to understand this notion of content and process subjects. Halliday (1982) says that when we use language, we *learn language,* we *learn through language* and we *learn about language.* According to Jaggar and Smith-Burke (1985), Halliday emphasises two more things:

> *All three processes take place side by side, reinforcing each other, and are largely* subconscious. *All three are* social *processes. They are learned in meaningful communication with others.(p. 3)*

From a learner's point of view, integration takes place in a similar subconscious and social way. Our goal is to aid this process.

In the integrated framework proposed here, students *learn language* in a vast range of contexts. It is difficult to think of an activity in which learners would not be using oral language, and there would be many instances where written language is the medium for recording ideas and information. In this sense, students are using language to construct and represent their ideas about the topic under investigation. They are also *learning through language,* although the ideas (facts, concepts and generalisations) being considered are not part of the language curriculum. These ideas (about the environment, life cycles, technology, energy, families and cultures) are fundamental to the subjects listed above as content subjects. The suggestion is that students are using language to learn about the content of these other subjects. Similarily, we can use art to learn

Six-year-old Sharon represents her shadow.

about social education or mathematics to learn about science.

When the focus shifts to the explicit study of the structure or conventions of language, students are *learning about language*. The objectives of the language program provide the major focus for learning and, in this sense, the students are studying language rather than the integrated unit.

A MODEL OF INTEGRATED LEARNING

Information	Nature of activity	Subjects involved
Facts	*Prior knowledge* • making prediction • asking questions	
	Shared experience • observation • collecting information/data	*Learning about* • social education • science • environmental education • personal development • technolody studies
Concepts	*Processing information* • listing • grouping • categorising • classifying • labelling • organising ideas	*Learning through* • language • art • drama • mathematics • movement • music
Generalisations	*Synthesising* • making statements • generalising • looking for relationships	*Learning about* • social education • science • environmental education • personal development • technology studies
Further information	*Refinement and extension of knowledge* • elaborating • justifying • reflecting	

Figure 1.2: A model of integrated learning

Two curriculum activities provide an illustration of the relationship between content and process. When constructing models of spiders, learners use concepts, skills and conventions which are developed through the art curriculum, in order to represent their understandings of the features of spiders. In this example, art is being used to represent ideas from science. Similarly, the reading of Katherine Paterson's *The Great Gilly Hopkins* as part of the language curriculum inevitably raises important ideas about child/adult relationships and identity which we usually associate with the social education curriculum. In this sense, the *content* of these two activities could be classified as science and social education although the ideas are being expressed through art and language.

Integrating the curriculum involves the selection of content topics from the content subjects, and the development or refinement of student knowledge of this content through the application of concepts and skills developed in the process subjects.

Content must always drive our planning. We need to ask:

- What will students be learning about (the chosen topic) by participating in this activity?

WHAT IS SIGNIFICANT CONTENT

Some approaches to the content subjects have resulted in the trivialisation of knowledge. The focus has been on the transmission of discrete facts from particular subject areas. Facts learned in a transmission model can become overloaded and rarely remembered. This has been typified by the memorising of particular dates, events and people rather than the factors which made these things significant.

Content in an integrated approach relates to the broader understandings about the world that are significant, transferable and able to be generalised. Schooling must address the issues of significance and this can begin in the earliest years of formal education:

> *To function effectively in society and to sustain or improve the quality of life, people need to focus on things which are really important. They need to understand themselves and others. They need to develop their own potential. They need to make connections. It is not enough to be simply interested or amused. It is possible, however, to be interested and amused by the important. (Newell & Stubbs 1990, p. 16)*

This engagement with challenging and important ideas became an issue with a group of teachers at Eltham East Primary School.

> *I have been amazed at how interested the Prep children are in the topics and how much they know. They could tell me the different sorts of dinosaurs and how we can identify them. This made us change some of the planned understandings to make them more sophisticated. We are now doing a topic on the solar system. They knew the names of all the planets and how big they were. It's been fascinating for me to watch them share what they know. (Lorraine Gamble)*

Lorraine went on to discuss the way that the team of teachers planned important ideas, the benefits of the approach, and the need for it to be implemented across the whole school:

> *It's really good to plan this way. We all sit down and think about the ideas that we want the children to learn. It's important that the whole school plans this way.*

Brachiosaurus was the tallest dinosaur.

A five-year-old's investigation of dinosaurs.

There are nine planets in the solar system.

The prior knowledge of a group of five-year-olds about the solar system.

If Prep children are given the opportunity to learn the important and challenging ideas, they need to continue with this approach later in the school. Once we have challenged them they easily get bored with just learning skills.

The issues of whole-school planning and teacher change are very important to the implementation of an integrated approach. They are explored in detail in chapter 6.

THE DIFFERENCES BETWEEN INTEGRATED AND THEMATIC APPROACHES TO LEARNING

Integrated curriculum units form only part of the total learning program. We also need to provide quality programs in language, music, art, drama, mathematics and physical education. These process subjects deal with concepts, skills and conventions which are best developed within their own conceptual frameworks, although there may be 'teachable moments' where a particular skill can be introduced in an integrated context.

When preparing a weekly program, we need to plan some activities for a planned integrated curriculum unit and others which will meet the various subject requirements of the curriculum. Specific skills and concepts critical to many subjects will be developed either by the classroom or specialist teachers in the context of those particular subjects. There will be specific language sessions where the focus is principally on language. For example, learning to write factual reports as part of the language program may involve analysing a range of different reports, jointly constructing texts using a range of topics and exploring the conventions which are part of this particular form of writing. Analysis may include newspaper reports, medical reports, school reports, as well as the scientific reports which are used to write about the natural and physical world. In an art program, students might explore texture which would involve paint, paper and natural materials.

The ideas and skills developed in these specific subject areas can also be applied in future integrated curriculum units so that reports could be written about amphibians, or ecosystems could be visually represented using a variety of textures. The issues in planning a language program to accompany integrated units are explored in more detail in chapter 4.

An example of a weekly program incorporating an integrated unit is shown on pages 14–15.

In an integrated curriculum unit *all* activities contain opportunities for students to learn more about the content. At the same time, such activities must allow students to represent their developing ideas through one or more of the process subjects in the curriculum. Because of this, many good activities don't qualify as integrated activities. If a poem, song or story does not enable students to learn social or scientific information, it does not meet these criteria for integration. By all means teach 'Frog Went Walking on a Summer Day' as part of the music program, but let's not pretend that students are learning significant ideas about frogs when they sing this song! Similarly, activities such as counting imaginary frogs may improve students' one-to-one correspondence but no matter how many frogs you count, your knowledge of them remains the same. Much of what is inappropriate in an integrated context can be very worthwhile as part of the music, language or maths program.

In this conceptual framework, the use of flow charts containing loosely correlated activities (often in the form of songs, stories or poems) would *not* qualify as an integrated approach. Such activities dilute the content to a point where students cannot further their knowledge of the subject and in an integrated approach, each activity should provide students with opportunities to learn more about the topic. In the main, the use of flow charts characterises what can best be called a thematic approach.

The limitation of thematic approaches is that they do not help us to plan in ways which maximise opportunities for students to make the connections. This is revealed in the following teacher comment:

> *I now see that I have been starting in the wrong way. I always started with a flow chart and made arrows to my curriculum areas to relate them to the topic. This new way of planning makes me start with the big ideas about the topic first. Once I have these ideas sorted out, the curriculum activities become more interesting to plan. (Len Vardy)*

THE CHARACTERISTICS OF INTEGRATED LEARNING

Authentic integration takes place in the mind of the learner. The quest for meaning is fundamental. As learners pursue their investigations, the knowledge of a topic unfolds like the hues of a paint chart, leading to increased density of understanding rather than a scrambled colour mosaic. This process takes time. Refinement and modification of knowledge

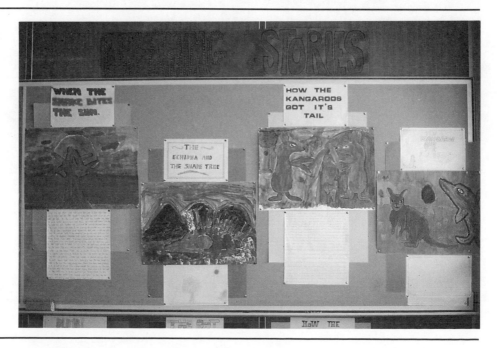

Students investigating Aboriginal culture.

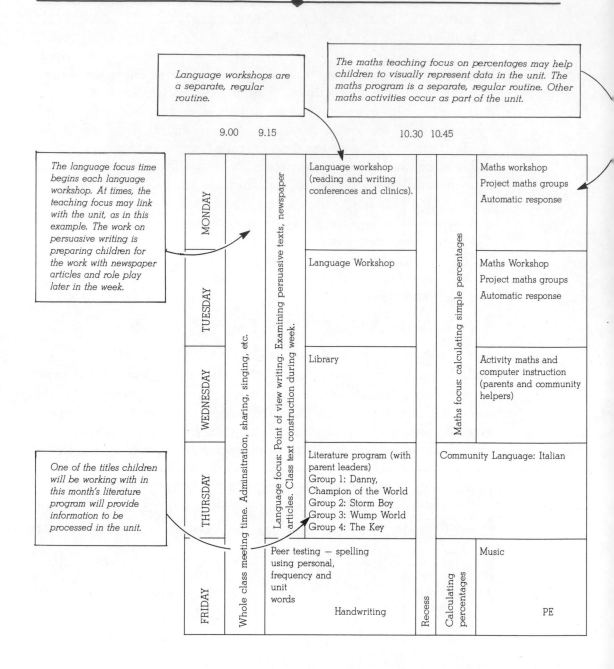

Figure 1.3: Timetable for week 3 of 'The Changing Environment'. Regular routines, such as specialists, maths and language workshops would remain fixed each week. The content of unit sessions would vary from week to week.

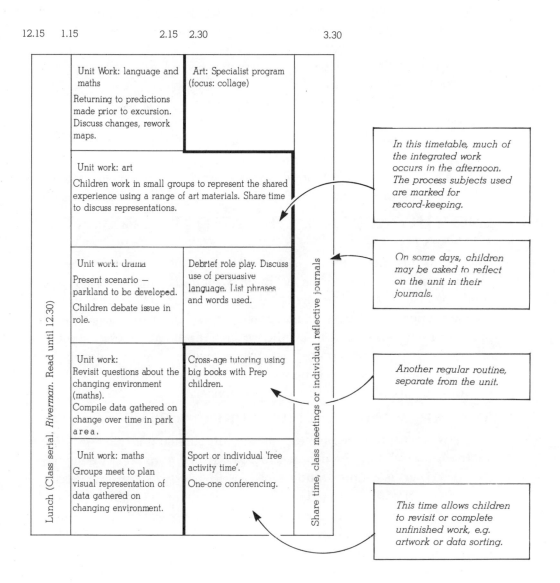

12.15   1.15   2.15   2.30   3.30

Lunch (Class serial. *Riverman*. Read until 12.30)

Unit Work: language and maths

Returning to predictions made prior to excursion. Discuss changes, rework maps.

Art: Specialist program (focus: collage)

Unit work: art

Children work in small groups to represent the shared experience using a range of art materials. Share time to discuss representations.

Unit work: drama

Present scenario — parkland to be developed.
Children debate issue in role.

Debrief role play. Discuss use of persuasive language. List phrases and words used.

Unit work:
Revisit questions about the changing environment (maths).
Compile data gathered on change over time in park area.

Cross-age tutoring using big books with Prep children.

Unit work: maths
Groups meet to plan visual representation of data gathered on changing environment.

Sport or individual 'free activity time'.
One-one conferencing.

Share time, class meetings or individual reflective journals

In this timetable, much of the integrated work occurs in the afternoon. The process subjects used are marked for record-keeping.

On some days, children may be asked to reflect on the unit in their journals.

Another regular routine, separate from the unit.

This time allows children to revisit or complete unfinished work, e.g. artwork or data sorting.

requires sustained periods of investigation or exploration, analysis or judgement, and reasons for returning with additional questions. Thus, an integrated program demands longer blocks of time to allow learners these opportunities.

Integrated curriculum units are planned to allow students to:

- develop understandings through sustained interaction, conversation or discussion about concepts, ideas, values and modes of presenting information
- develop an understanding of the variety of ways in which we can present, represent and transform ideas about the world
- build on and extend their personal, out-of-school experiences and knowledge
- understand the difference between real-world, factual experiences and exploration of knowledge, and fictional imagined worlds
- develop a sense of reflection about their world and their environment which leads to action, control and conservation.

INQUIRY APPROACH AND INTEGRATED LEARNING

Integral to this model of integrated learning is the general approach to teaching and learning known as **inquiry**. Inquiry approaches provide conditions which allow learners to take control of their learning, to build on their prior knowledge, to make and test predictions, to gather and organise information and to synthesise their findings. These conditions encourage risk-taking, approximation, the exploration of patterns and relationships, reflection on experience, and an understanding of differing interests, points of view and value positions.

TOWARDS HOLISITIC APPROACHES

Concern about the fragmented nature of curriculum has prompted approaches which have brought together knowledge from areas traditionally considered in isolation. Studies of science, technology and society, environmental education, and personal development exemplify this trend. Teaching and learning strategies such as co-operative learning, genre-based language, whole language and whole maths have been prominent and influential in shaping our classroom programs.

The concept of integrated learning can be seen as complementary to these trends and developments. They can all be seen as responses to previous developments which have resulted in the fragmentation of the curriculum. There are also many philosophical assumptions and beliefs about learning which are shared by these approaches and the research bases on which they have been constructed share many common roots.

There are, of course, significant differences. Co-operative learning has focused our attention on the important role of talk in sharing and clarifying ideas. Genre-based language has stressed the importance of content (or field) and the functions of language in a contemporary society. Whole language has provided an emphasis on context and process for the acquisition of skills and has addressed the problem of fragmenting language into separate subjects in the curriculum. Whole maths has moved towards a problem-solving approach which addresses real-life situations.

All these approaches are characterised by the sharing of responsibility by the teacher and the learners, a redefinition of the role of the teacher and an emphasis on students making decisions about the subject of their investigations and the communication and presentation of information. The integrated approach outlined here offers the best features of each of these developments together with opportunities for learners to employ many of the concepts and skills they have developed in the traditional subjects.

THE NEED FOR STRUCTURE

The term *structure* often has negative connotations associated with control: prescription, closed questions, teacher-directed outcomes or projects. However, in a school context, successful learning environments need a structure. The challenge lies in developing a structure which offers support for the learner but which allows opportunities for outcomes or directions which we have not necessarily anticipated. A supportive structure is a pre-requisite for *authentic negotiation* between the teacher and the learners. An effective structure will reflect our knowledge and organisation, and provide predictable routines and ways of working for the learners.

Three students learning co-operatively.

The structure of predictable routines in integrated curriculum units includes:

- the framework of the planning model
- the organisation of the format of the sessions (individual/small group/whole class) and appropriate seating arrangements
- provision of a range of grouping strategies (individual, pairs, small groups, large groups, whole class)
- opportunities to reflect upon learning, share and rehearse for the next session or activity
- opportunities for learners to negotiate what they will investigate and how they will present or report their findings.

Within these predictable routines there is an expectation that unpredictable (creative) learning behaviour will occur. Teachers and learners need structure. The suggested structure provides opportunities to cater for equality of opportunity, individual differences, different interests and abilities, diversity of learning outcomes and tolerance of different world views, values and attitudes. It also allows teachers and learners to make sense of their school day.

2

A PLANNING MODEL

Keith Pigdon and **Marilyn Woolley** provide a planning model which shows explicitly the relationship and interdependence of curriculum content and process. A rationale for the specific components of the planning model and the sequences within and between them is also provided. Inherent in the model is a view of learning which aims to extend and refine students' developing knowledge of the world and increase their capacity to take social action.

Integrating students' learning involves the bringing together of many curriculum components. To do this effectively, a planning model for the development of integrated curriculum units is necessary. The planning model used here breaks down the task into a number of smaller more manageable components. It also provides a sequence for us to follow. The sequence involves the teacher planning activities which begin with the learner's prior knowledge. The unit is based around a **shared experience**, planned by the teacher, through which learners gather new information about the topic. This shared experience is designed to take learners beyond their existing knowledge. It represents a deliberate intervention in the learning cycle and relies on teachers having carefully considered and documented what it is they want the learners to know about that topic. However, the classroom activities are highly interactive and students have many opportunities to influence directions and determine outcomes. The shared experience is followed by a series of activities which allow students to sort out the information and represent their ideas and interpretations. These activities deliberately move from visual to more abstract modes of expression.

The planning model helps the teacher decide what to teach, how to teach it, and how to sequence sessions in order to help students form opinions, synthesise, and summarise the essential ideas. As the teacher moves through the planning cycle, decisions about the most appropriate grouping for a particular activity become critical to successful implementation. The framework provided is a model for planning and a model for action and reflection.

A PROGRAM LEVEL PLANNING
1 Selection of a topic for the unit
2 Writing specific understandings for the unit

B ACTIVITY LEVEL PLANNING
3 Tuning in
4 The shared experience
5 Sorting out the shared experience
   (a) Art activities
   (b) Drama activities
   (c) Maths activities
   (d) Language activities
   (e) Generalisations
6 Related experiences
7 Sorting out the related experiences
8 Values clarification
9 Reflection and action

C RECORD KEEPING AND EVALUATION
10 Evaluation of the teaching strategies and materials
11 Evaluation of the learner's development
12 Future planning

PLANNING FOR IMPLEMENTATION
SELECTION OF A TOPIC

Topics for integrated curriculum units emerge from the content subjects. Curriculum guidelines for social education, science, environmental education and personal development provide the basis from which to select topics and devise understandings for the unit. Students can also be involved in decisions about topic selection. Topics should be selected and sequenced in ways that allow learners to explore connection between the content areas.

All topics should have a clear focus. Decisions about topics should take these considerations into account:
- areas which have been explored by the students during the current and previous years
- the school's existing curriculum, general community considerations and significant current and historical events
- the availability of appropriate shared experiences which will play a central role in the development of the topic. These may include excursions, visitors to the classroom, bringing living things and objects into the classroom, films, videotapes, pictures, and books
- student interest in a particular area.

SPECIFIC UNDERSTANDINGS FOR THE UNIT

Once we have determined a topic to provide a focus for teaching and learning, we should then consider and list the specific understandings about the world which students may gain from exploring that content.

These understandings are usually expressed as generalised statements, giving our planning greater purpose and direction because they provide us with criteria for the selection of resources and guidelines for choice of activities and experiences. Furthermore, they should become the focal point for our evaluation and future planning.

The specific understandings may relate to a more general set of ideas which the school uses as the basis for developing its content subjects. When planning these specific understandings, we make systematic attempts to develop and refine students' ideas. It is a process which begins in the first year of school and progresses throughout a learner's formal education. These understandings help to provide the framework by which schooling can take students beyond the knowledge they gather in their own personal lives.

When writing specific understandings, we should ask these questions:

Is this statement about the world:

- true or valid?
- worth knowing?
- appropriate to the needs, interests, experiences and cultural backgrounds of the students?
- likely to take the students beyond their present experience and understanding?

The specific understandings help us to be more explicit about the knowledge base of the unit and to further define the parameters of the topic. Two distinctively different examples written for the topic 'Transport' are provided to illustrate this point. The first was written for a Year 5/6 class in an inner suburban school. This unit has a clear environmental and social class focus.

TRANSPORT

1 Some forms of transport have significantly altered the landscape.
2 Some forms of transport have significantly damaged the natural environment.
3 In modern cities there may be a conflict between the demand for private transportation and the need for an effective public transport system.
4 The types of transport used in the twentieth century have placed huge demands on the precious and finite fossil fuel reserves which are being depleted rapidly.
5 In most societies, people do not have equal access to all forms of transport.
6 There are relationships between the lifestyles of citizens, the transport system, and the economic system.

The second example was written for a Year 1/2 group of students in a newer outer suburban area. The unit has more of a people and work focus.

TRANSPORT
1 Transport can be classed into three main categories — land, sea, and air.
2 Transport has changed over the years.
3 Specialised people are associated with the transport industry.
4 Vehicles have many attributes: wheels, engine, carrying capacity, speed, noise, etc.
5 Transport meets a variety of individual and business needs.
6 We can learn basic ideas about people through transport.

At this stage, these specific understandings are for teacher use and reference. They may be shared with the learners at a later stage after learners have written their own generalisations.

While these understandings underpin our choice of resources and activities, they should not be seen as fixed or inflexible. We make certain assumptions about the knowledge, interests and needs of learners which sometimes prove to be inaccurate. In the early stages of the unit, it may become clear that one or more of these understandings is either too sophisticated or insufficiently challenging for a group of learners. They may need to change in response to new perspectives introduced by the students, other staff, parents or community members. We must be prepared to adapt our original plans to make them more appropriate to our learners.

Once the specific understandings have been written, it is time to decide on an appropriate shared experience.

THE SHARED EXPERIENCE

PURPOSES
An appropriate shared experience can:
(i)   further stimulate the students' curiosity
(ii)   provide new information which may answer some of their early questions
(iii) raise other questions for them to explore in the future
(iv)   challenge their knowledge, beliefs and values
(v)   help students to make sense of further activities and experiences which have been planned for them.

A shared experience is a planned activity in which the whole class participates. It may take the form of an excursion, watching a videotape or film, observing a set of pictures, listening to or interviewing a guest speaker, observing animals or plants in a classroom, being read to from a large format information book or listening to an audiotape. It involves the teacher selecting a resource or place to visit which is rich in information about the topic. The information available to learners through the shared experience should relate closely to the specific understandings.

Any shared experience fulfils a vital function in the development of a unit by linking and broadening the diverse background experiences and understandings which students bring to any topic. This is the stage of the unit when students encounter new information. The shared experience needs to provide rich information and new perspectives which will challenge *all* students to refine and *extend* their current knowledge of a topic.

We can also take the opportunity to extend students' experiential base through the careful choice of locations and materials for this aspect of the unit. The broadening of students experience is surely one of the most compelling justifications for compulsory schooling, and a way in which we can demonstrate our accountability to the community.

Direct experiences in the form of excursions, camps, walking visits to places around the community, visitors to the school, living things and objects brought into the classroom are valuable because they involve students in face-to-face encounters with reality.

Vicarious experiences, such as stimulus pictures and experiential films, may have the advantage of being available for further reference and re-examination. There are also things of significance to students which cannot be experienced directly at school. Books are more appropriately used later in the unit, unless rich pictorial information can be presented in big book format and shared by the class.

There may be occasions when multiple shared experiences are appropriate or where the shared experience extends over a period of time. Incubating chickens as a shared experience is one such example.

Just as the experiences which friends share help to sustain their friendships, shared experiences provide a foundation for sustaining interest in a topic over an extended period of time. Shared experiences also contribute to a sense of community as students exchange their developing ideas about a topic and reflect on the experiences they have had together.

TUNING IN

PURPOSES
The tuning-in stage aims to:
(i)   provide students with opportunities to become engaged with the topic
(ii) find out what the students already know about the topic
(iii) allow students to share their personal experience of the topic
(iv) ascertain the students' initial curiosity about the topic
(v)   provide students with a focus for the forthcoming shared experience
(vi) help in the planning of further experiences and activities.

Students bring a vast range of experience to school. At the tuning in stage we need to think about how we can take advantage of the diversity of students' personal experience and life styles; how we can evaluate what the students already know about the topic and how we can find out what they want to know about it. During activities which allow students to share and exchange their prior knowledge, we gain insights into students' conceptions (and misconceptions) about particular ideas, and the strength or sophistication of their existing knowledge. In some cases, the sources of their ideas also become apparent (direct experience, television, other family members or friends

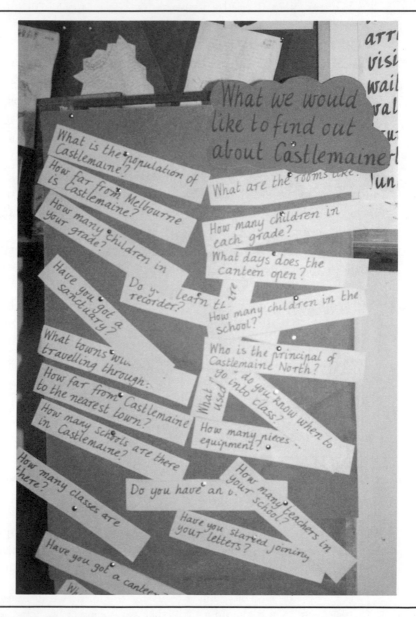

Student questions about Castlemaine.

or reading), along with information which helps us to plan additional activities to give new or different perspectives on the students' developing knowledge.

Students in Kath Murdoch's Year 3/4 class at Williamstown Primary were setting up the room to house some lizards. They were asked what questions they had about lizards. These were some responses:

QUESTIONS WE HAVE ABOUT LIZARDS
1 What lizards are wild? What lizards are tame? (Leanne)
2 Do all lizards lie in the sun to get warm? (Aaron)
3 What do lizards eat? (Adam)
4 Which lizards drop their tails? (Jimmy)
5 How often do lizards eat? (Ben)
6 Do all lizards look the same? (Adele)
7 What things eat lizards? (Ben)
8 How do lizards have babies? (Ingrid)
9 Why do lizards lose their tails? (Rachael)

Their questions reveal a range of curiosities, interests and knowledge. Aaron had information to share: *Do all lizards lie in the sun to get warm?* and Ben was interested in food for lizards and lizards as food: *How often do lizards eat? What things eat lizards?*

At other times, students may be asked to tell what they already know about a topic in response to a particular focus question. Cheryl Semple and Ann Burke were planning to incubate chicken eggs as a shared experience for their unit on chickens in their Brunswick Primary classroom. They asked the students this question:
• How does the chicken hatch?
These were some of the responses they recorded:

---

1 The egg gets smaller so the chicken breaks out.
2 The chicken gets bigger.
3 The chicken kicks the egg to get out.
4 The chicken pecks the egg with its beak.
5 The chicken keeps making the hole until it is big enough for it to get out.

Each of these statements represents an explanation. Once these explanations are known, we may be able to devise ways for students to test them. For example, the first statement could be tested by having the student select an egg, mark it for identification, and take regular measurements of it to discover whether it does get smaller.

Identifying the sources and nature of students' prior knowledge can sometimes allow us to devise strategies that will demonstrate to students that they have misconceptions or have become confused.

Sometimes we should set specific tasks for students to carry out

Measuring the growth of chickens.

during the shared experience which will involve them in data collection of some kind. Students may design their own observation tasks based on the questions and statements they generated earlier in this stage. You may want to allocate particular focus questions for different groups, e.g. What do lizards eat? Which lizards drop their tails? Why do lizards lie in the sun?

Activities which involve students in observation are much more effective than the barrage of information which they sometimes receive during the course of guided excursions. If this component is to be effective, students must have a clear sense of purpose about why they are gathering information.

SORTING OUT THE SHARED EXPERIENCE

PURPOSES

These activities aim to:
(i) provide students with concrete means of sorting out and representing information and ideas arising from the shared experience
(ii) provide a focus for oral language exchanges which flow from the shared experience
(iii) allow students to express their ideas through visual formats
(iv) allow for a range of diverse outcomes

This is a critical component of the unit where students work through the observations and ideas gathered during the shared experience. This is done by planning activities that allow students to talk and think about

Reporting back to the class.

the experience, to interpret and organise the information they have gathered, and to represent and test their developing understandings.

We must attempt to cater for difference in as many ways as we can manage. This does not mean that all students need to be working at something different. It does mean that there can be different choices and outcomes for different learners, that there will be a range of grouping strategies to suit the various tasks, and that there will be a variety of outlets through which students can express themselves.

SELECTING THE CURRICULUM AREAS

The selection of suitable curriculum areas for sorting out the shared experience will depend on the kind of information gathered by the students and the initial understandings. There is no need to feel that *all* the process subjects must be involved in each unit. The choice depends on the understandings driving the unit and the nature of the information. For example, there will be times when mathematics is inappropriate and others when movement and dance have little to contribute.

SORTING OUT THE INFORMATION VISUALLY

Many children are good visual thinkers. They find it easier to express their ideas visually than through language. Initial clarification and expression of ideas through a visual medium may also help them to use written language later on. During a variety of art and construction activities, learners have many opportunities to offer, exchange, defend and clarify ideas gathered during the shared experience. Visual records

A visual record of a zoo excursion.

Acting out telephone communication.

are both colourful and concrete and, when displayed, provide students with a sustained reference for comparison of ideas and viewpoints. They can demonstrate to parents the quality of information gathered and the benefits of shared experiences (which may involve a financial cost) to the classroom learning program. These records can be referred to throughout the unit for the purpose of labelling, listing or the compilation of tables or retrieval charts related to the topic.

SORTING OUT INFORMATION USING DRAMA, MOVEMENT OR MUSIC

Drama offers opportunities to shift the focus of a unit towards the social consequences of events. Students need to understand that people have different values, attitudes and opinions as a result of their different experiences. Drama, role play, movement and dance activities can help to develop positive attitudes towards the exchange of different values and perspectives and to foster a tolerance of difference and a deeper understanding of one's own behaviour.

SORTING OUT INFORMATION MATHEMATICALLY

Mathematics can be a powerful way of organising, representing and understanding information. The type of information gathered during the shared experience usually determines the usefulness of mathematics as a processing medium. Quantitative information is well suited to this type of activity. Students may need to apply their knowledge of numbers, fractions, measurement, spatial relations, visual represent- ation, decimals and percentages to analyse their data. Mathematical processing involves estimating, hypothesising, generalising, justifying, describing and explaining. It also engages learners in making decisions about the most effective means to show patterns and relationships using graphs, tables or diagrams.

SORTING OUT INFORMATION USING WRITTEN LANGUAGE

Once students have had the opportunity to talk through and clarify their ideas using some or all of the above processing mechanisms, they

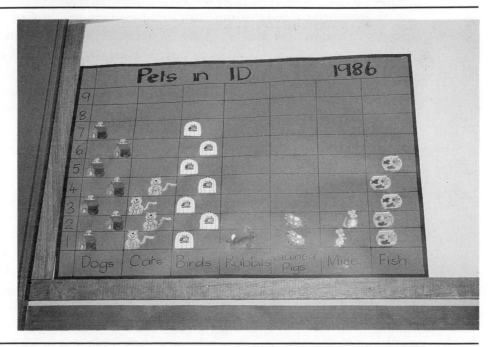

Graphing family pets.

can then generalise about the topic using written language. This sequencing of activities allows students to rehearse their intended meanings before committing them to paper. These generalisations can form the basis of written reports, explanations and arguments. By using a simple focus question: *What can we now say or tell others about___ ?*, we can encourage students to generate several statements. These can be drafted on large sheets or strips and displayed for conferencing about clarity of meaning, accuracy and perspective.

Sally Dayton's and Paul Molyneux's Year 4-6 class at Boundary Road, North Melbourne Primary made these statements:

WHAT WE KNOW ABOUT MAGNETS
1   We use magnets to make electric appliances (like telephones and radios) work.
2   Magnets are useful for picking up iron and steel objects.
3   Magnets work through water, plastic, glass, wood and paper.
4   A magnet can be used as a compass. It always points north.
5   Two north poles or two south poles repel.
6   Opposite poles attract.
7   The first magnet was a stone found near Magnesium in what is now Turkey.

These statements can then be organised and classified into particular categories of information with suitable headings and appropriate titles. In terms of knowledge, these generalisations may highlight gaps or inconsistencies and demonstrate the need for further research or investigation through a range of related experiences. In terms of language, they can also signal the need for specific activities (for individuals or groups) dealing with the use of conventions, syntax or text organisation and spelling. Draft generalisations can be cut up for sentence recomposition or used as the basis for cloze activities or word study and analysis.

A wider range of language activities is explored in chapter 4.

RELATED EXPERIENCES

PURPOSES
These experiences aim to:
(i)   extend the unit (if appropriate) in more specific directions as a result of insights gained from the shared experience
(ii)   provide more information in order to broaden the range of understandings available to the students.

As the unit proceeds, learners' ideas and understandings will continue to develop. They may now be able to make sense of a wider range of related experiences, which can be offered at an individual, small group or class level. Students may negotiate personal or group areas of interest. Related experiences should challenge and extend the knowledge base of learners.

They usually take the form of information books, and short videos or films. The information in related experiences may relate to the specific understandings but it often explores wider issues. A unit on chickens may develop in a number of different directions to include aspects such as battery farming techniques, the concept of incubation, or other life cycles.

When selecting books for related experiences, we should make sure that students see how ideas about the world are represented in a range of factual genres including reports, enquiries, explanations, expositions, procedures and narrative information. Factual texts show the integration of social and scientific information with language, art, graphs, tables, charts, maps and mathematical concepts and provide important models for students' writing. Good models are now available (some in big-book form for older students). Some picture storybooks are developed around significant social concepts and they raise important issues and values questions.

At this stage of the unit, students and teachers may return to their initial statements developed during the tuning in sessions to review their earlier knowledge, predictions and questions.

SORTING OUT RELATED EXPERIENCES

Related experiences may be processed through similar activities to those suggested for the shared experience. Once again, the purpose of the activity and the nature of the information should determine the process subject areas involved. At the conclusion of this sequence of activities we should encourage students to return to their generalisations formulated after the shared experience with a view to refining and elaborating them.

After studying their own community, students in Ian Holton's Year 3 class at Deer Park North Primary made these generalisations:

WHAT WE THINK A COMMUNITY IS
1 A place where people live.
2 A part of a country.
3 A place where people work.
4 A place with shops.
5 Every community has a milk bar.
6 A place where people do business with other people.
7 There is always a petrol station in a community.

After a shift in focus through related experience, which had them studying ant communities they revised their generalisations.

WHAT DO WE THINK NOW?
1 All living things live in a community.
2 Things living together have jobs.
3 Things fight to protect their community.
4 Things share facilities and services.

VALUES CLARIFICATION

Teaching about the social and physical world does far more than develop facts, concepts and generalisations. It also allows exploration of values and attitudes about the way the world works. As teachers, we need to identify our own values and attitudes about topics we are teaching and be aware of the ways these values may influence our choice of activity, selection of material or our responses to students.

Similarly, students develop and clarify their own values and attitudes as they learn more about the world. This clarification is best achieved through exposure to, and comparison of, the range of beliefs that are held by different people and groups of people in society.

There will be different perspectives — including multicultural, gender, Aboriginal and global — from which knowledge can be viewed. However, it is equally important for students to understand that, within these perspectives, there will be a wide variety of values, beliefs, interests, customs and power relationships which govern notions of participation, justice and equity, freedom and tolerance, rights and responsibilities, participation and social action, and which underpin the political, economic, cultural and social practices in our and other societies. Students also need to discuss the role of media and technology in shaping our perception and perspectives.

In an integrated approach there are many opportunities to encourage students to reflect on and articulate their values and those of others. There will be different perspectives. Such opportunities arise through the following sorts of activities:

- Class or small group discussion about issues.
- How do you feel about that? Why?
- Co-operative group work where students must share and clarify views about a particular problem.
- Role play where students are asked to take on the role of someone who feels differently from the way they do.
- Use of media (e.g. film) and the analysis of that media:
  What do you think is the main message in this video?
  Who is the message aimed at?
  Who might have made the video?
  How would . . . do it differently?

During the unit, it is important that students' and teachers' feelings about issues are recognised, articulated, recorded and valued.

REFLECTION AND ACTION

PURPOSES

This stage of the unit aims to:

(i)   empower students and help develop the belief that they can be effective participants in society

(ii) help students to make links between their understandings and their experience in the real world

(iii) provide further insight into students' understandings for future unit planning.

Taking action allows students to put their knowledge and ideas into a practical and concrete form. As they reflect on what they have learnt, students may develop concerns about, or interests in, particular issues. The action component of the integrated unit involves students in considering what can be done about those issues.

Implementing a course of action should develop a sense of empowerment in students — the feeling thay they can do something to effect change in their world. It should be a positive experience. Students are engaged in planning, decision making and organising, and are developing the skills and attitudes that will enable them to become successful participants in society.

The form of action taken will depend largely on the topic. Some topics will lend themselves to action within the classroom, others to action in the school or the wider community. A unit on rules and responsibilities could lead to changes in classroom rules and sanctions. A unit on packaging could lead to suggestions to change the products available in the tuck shop, or to letters being sent to manufacturers.

Any action will need to be considered in terms of its purpose, and the time and resources available. Students should be encouraged to devise ways of monitoring and evaluating the success of their action.

RECORD KEEPING AND EVALUATION

It is important for students to accumulate concrete records of their learning and achievements throughout the unit. They can use these later as a reference point for additional questions, comparisons or for synthesising ideas. These records will take the form of individual, group and class files, lists, charts, tables, graphs, statements of generalisation, summaries, answers to questions and writing samples.

As the unit develops, some records will become dispensable as the information is transformed or refined. Others (such as files of samples of work) will serve as cumulative records of growth and progress.

Opportunities to talk, discuss and report to others develops students' reflective or metacognitive awareness of their own learning and the role of others in this learning. At the end of the unit, structured questions can help to synthesise these cognitive and social aspects.

- What did I learn about _____ ?
- What did I learn from working with others?
- What did I learn about working with others?

We can use a variety of techniques to accumulate information about students' progress and the effectiveness of the integrated unit. Information gathered from these records will help future planning.

The techniques selected will depend on the purposes of the activities, the nature of the shared and related experiences, and the content of the understandings. They include:

- observation
- anecdotal notes
- files of students' work (e.g. concept maps)
- student self-assessment
- journals
- checklists (e.g. co-operative group skills, problem solving skills)
- conferencing with students

EVALUATION OF THE TEACHING STRATEGIES AND MATERIALS

We also need to structure questions so that we can reflect systematically upon and improve our teaching strategies, and our selection and use of resources. We need to ask ourselves:

- Did my questions encourage a range of responses and possible alternatives?
- How did I allow for students to work with a range of other learners?
- Did my resources allow for sufficient clarification of issues and values?
- Did my resources demonstrate sufficient diversity, points of view and perspectives?
- Did I make the purposes of the activities clear to the learners?
- Did I allow time for student talk?
- Did I encourage risk taking and exploration of ideas?
- Did I provide time for student reflection and self-assessment?

EVALUATING THE LEARNER'S DEVELOPMENT

The major task here is to develop systematic ways of observing individual students, and collecting and recording the indicators of their progress. These will include:

- developing confidence and independence
- increasing knowledge of ideas and concepts (content)
- participation and engagement in actitivities
- application of inquiry skills and processes

- broadening repertoire of modes of presentation
- broadening repertoire of writing genres
- the growth of ability to reflect upon what has been learned, make comparisons, see alternatives
- development of collaborative and co-operative skills
- ability to reflect on and assess their own progress

FUTURE PLANNING

Evaluation is an ongoing and integral part of the planning process outlined in this model. It involves observation of student learning, together with a reconsideration of the specific understandings, the teaching strategies, the materials used, the learning environment and samples of students' work. Evaluation enables us to decide what sort of feedback is appropriate for the individual learner and also provides information to help us with future planning. The issues involved in assessment and evaluation are explored in more detail in chapter 5.

3
TRANSLATING THE MODEL INTO PRACTICE

Kath Murdoch uses the framework provided by the planning model to develop a range of activities and strategies which could be considered when planning integrated curriculum units. Using the topic 'The Changing Environment', she provides a range of resources, and a sequence of teaching/learning strategies which indicate clear purposes and outcomes. This provides options for teachers, to consider when implementing or adapting this integrated learning framework in their own unit planning and classroom settings.

◆

The following outline was developed for Year 3-4 students but could be adapted for both upper and lower levels.

A broad range of possibilities has been provided for each component. It is not envisaged that *all* the activities outlined for any component would be implemented within a particular unit.

A PROGRAM LEVEL PLANNING

1 SELECTION OF A TOPIC
The Changing Environment

2 UNDERSTANDINGS
- The natural environment is constantly changing.
- There are a range of factors which influence this change.
- Human beings have had an adverse impact on the natural environment.
- People and other animals depend on the natural environment for their survival.
- There are many things that we can do as individuals that will help reduce the stresses on the environment.
- People respond to the changing environment in different ways, but change ultimately affects us all.

B ACTIVITY LEVEL PLANNING

3 TUNING IN

PURPOSES

(i)   To provide students with opportunities to become engaged with the topic.
(ii)   To find out what the students already know about the topic.
(iii)   To allow students to share their personal experience of the topic.
(iv)   To ascertain the students' initial curiosity about the topic.
(v)   To provide students with a focus for the forthcoming shared experience.
(vi)   To help plan further experiences or activities.

The following activities are designed to fulfil **purpose (i).** They are simply ways to motivate and interest students in a new topic and provide background for the shared experience to follow. It may not be necessary to use these, as students may already be eager to begin exploring the topic.

(a) VISUALISATION

This works well in quiet, outdoor settings where students are not crowded together.

Ask the students to close their eyes and imagine that they are in the bush or some other natural area. You might want to read a description of a natural environment (for example, a passage from Colin Thiele's *Storm Boy*). Ask the students, 'What sounds can you hear? What can you see?' A tape of bush sounds may help to create the right atmosphere or provide an audio alternative. In small groups, students then share the things they imagined. They may also represent their ideas visually through art.

(b) SLIDES OR POSTERS

Display these as a stimulus for discussions about and reactions to the natural environment. Encourage students to bring books, posters, magazines, photographs, etc. to display in the classroom. Involve students in setting up display areas.

Resources such as these are available from the Australian Conservation Foundation or wilderness societies, zoo education services, state environment centres and Gould League centres.

(c) STORYTELLING

Teacher and students share their experiences of being in the natural environment . . . favourite places, memorable experiences, etc. Oral stories could be shared in a 'round the campfire' fashion at the end of the day. Favourite places could be plotted on a map of the state or country or represented through art.

Listening to taped stories and music.

(d) MUSIC

At this stage, songs can provide a stimulus for general discussion about characteristics of and feelings towards the natural environment.

Listen to some songs that describe the natural environment. There are tapes available from the Gould League e.g. *Environmental Song Book* or from state conservation departments. Many popular songs have been written about the environment. Write the words up on butcher's paper so that students can see them, listen to them and discuss.

The following activities help fulfil **purposes (ii)-(iv).** They give the teacher some idea of the students' prior knowledge, conceptual understandings and areas of interest.

(a) PROVIDE STUDENTS WITH A BROAD FOCUS QUESTION

What do you want to know about the natural environment?

Try to make sure that the task of writing down the questions does not limit the students' curiosity or thinking at this stage.

After some discussion, students may write their questions individually, in small groups, or as a class. Students who are unable to write their questions down may be able to get another student or teacher to do it for them.

These questions may be classified under headings or left as a general list. They should be returned to regularly when appropriate throughout the unit and may provide direction for individual, group and class investigations.

Label questions with students' names for future reference.

(b) PROVIDE A SPECIFIC FOCUS FOR DIFFERENT GROUPS

File written responses for future use and evaluation.

What do you know about the way people change the natural environment? What do you want to know about looking after the environment?

38

students may also keep records of their questions in individual books or folders.

(c) BRAINSTORM A BROAD IDEA

Ask students to consider the question, *What is a natural environment?*

Responses could be gathered through a whole class discussion or in small groups. Students may represent their ideas through writing or art.

(d) MAKE AN ENVIRONMENT WHEEL

Students draw a circle and divide it into four segments. In each segment they draw or write responses to the following statements:

Things in the natural environment that are abundant.
Things in the natural environment that are scarce.
Ways we harm the environment.
Ways we help the environment.

Students share their environment wheels.

Information is discussed, challenged and refined during the unit. The class could construct a giant environment wheel, to be added to during the unit.

(e) CONCEPT MAPPING

This is best done as an individual activity. You may need to model this first by using a different topic and constructing a map with the class.

Using key words about the changing environment, students prepare a draft concept map to illustrate their understandings. These words (approx 8–10) may be given by the teacher or generated by the learners themselves.

Write down ten words you think of when you think about the changing environment, then show the ways in which you think the words connect with one another.

Use word cards and Blu Tack so that the map can be changed at various stages in the unit. Students then share their maps. Statements of generalisation can be written from the map.

Concept mapping is further discussed in chapter 5.

(f) CONSTRUCTING MODELS

Models can be labelled for explanation.

In groups, students work out a way to make a model of a natural environment using a range of materials. *What do you need to show?* These models can be refined during the unit as students develop their understandings. You could ask groups of students to create different types of environments, for example, deserts, forests or wetlands.

(g) NEEDS AND WANTS

This may be done through a specific teaching session within the unit and is also an effective values clarification activity.

The difference between needs and wants is an important concept that students should explore early in the unit. In their efforts to satisfy their needs and wants, humans put pressure on the environment. Activities that require students to examine their *own* needs and wants are best, and could take place through listing, drawing, discussing and debating.

List 10 of your favourite items at home. Which do you need? Which are 'wants'?
How do we satisfy our needs and wants?
How do our needs and wants affect the environment?
Which have the most impact on the environment?

A class consensus should be reached on appropriate definitions of needs and wants. Discuss the question, *What are reasonable wants?*

(h) INTERVIEW ACTIVITIES: ONE-TO-ONE OR SMALL GROUP SURVEYS

Students are given the task of finding out what others know about a focus question or finding out what others want to know. Report back at a small group or class level.

The following approaches are some of the many that could be used to fulfil **purposes (v) and (vi).**

(a) DECIDING DIRECTIONS

At this stage students may write letters or visit libraries to begin investigations.

Having explored students' interests and prior knowledge, you may wish to involve them in deciding on ways to find out more about the topic. This is where negotiation can take place. You have already set down some of the ideas you believe to be of value in the specific understandings and now students are in a position to suggest directions in which they are interested. Often these will be similar to your own ideas.

One way to do this is to refer back to questions and areas of interest raised by students earlier in the tuning in stage and ask them to suggest ways in which information might be gained.

(b) INTERVIEWS

Students interview people about the place they are about to visit or about the topic of the video they are going to watch.

(c) MAPPING/DRAWING

These maps should be re-examined after the shared experience.

Students construct a map of the excursion area before visiting it. This may be a prediction activity, e.g. *What do you think it will look like?* or they may use information they have already gathered about the site.

(d) ORGANISING DATA COLLECTION OR FOCUS

Students may want to set tasks for themselves such as listing the questions to be answered or the activities they wish to carry out during the shared experience. These tasks may relate to the questions developed during the tuning in phase, e.g.

Listing evidence of human impact on the environment.

Noting the different ways the environment is protected.

Listing of all the natural and made things seen in the environment.

Interviewing people about changes in the particular area.

Students could prepare tally sheets or organise equipment for gathering data.

5 THE SHARED EXPERIENCE

> **PURPOSES**
>
> An appropriate shared experience can:
> (i) further stimulate the students' curiosity
> (ii) provide new information which may answer some of their early questions
> (iii) raise other questions for them to explore in the future
> (iv) challenge their knowledge, beliefs and values
> (v) help students to make sense of further activities and experiences which have been planned for them.

(a) VISITS

• **Visit a local, natural area** which has been adversely affected in some way, for example, a polluted creek, a littered park, or, alternatively, visit an area which is being regenerated.

Growing plants in the classroom.

Sidebar (left margin): Environmental measuring and observation techniques can be found in a range of environmental educational resource books.

- **Visit a local park.** Students may gather data on human impact on the environment as well as enjoying and observing a parkland setting.
- **Visit a bush setting,** a state or national park. Human impact may be less observable here but richer data on the natural environment could be gathered.

(b) INCURSIONS

- Visits to the school or classroom by representatives of environmental groups or by environmental education theatre companies.
- **Guest speakers** — the Australian Conservation Foundation or other environmental groups may be able to provide a guest speaker. People in the local community may come in and share their recollections of how a local area has changed.

Make sure that students prepare for this by formulating interview questions.

(c) FILM AND VIDEO

Select videos that explore environmental change, for example *The Lorax.* Many documentaries on the environment have been made for television over the last few years. Some are suitable for this age group. You should view them carefully to ensure that the ideas and concepts are accessible and relevant to the students and to your planned understandings.

Students should have a focus when watching the video, or be able to bring specific questions to it. Consider showing videos in sections, allowing for questioning and discussion along the way.

6 SORTING OUT THE SHARED EXPERIENCE

PURPOSES

(i)   To provide students with a concrete means of representing information and ideas arising from the shared experience.

(ii) To provide a focus for oral language exchanges which flow from the shared experience.

(iii) To allow students to express their ideas through visual formats.

(iv) To allow for a range of diverse outcomes.

As a first step you may wish to give students the opportunity to make some initial responses to the shared experience through group discussion or by returning to concrete records of their predictions.

(a) ART ACTIVITIES

1 Ask the students to focus on an aspect of the shared experience and to think about how this could be represented visually.

Show them the range of materials available. Tell them they now have three decisions to make.

Most of these activities can be done individually, in pairs, in small groups or as a whole class activity.

Giving learners responsibility.

- Which idea or aspect they would like to represent. (Ask them to share their ideas with others.)
- Would they prefer to work alone, in a pair, or in a small group?
- Which materials they would like to use.

Providing for differences in the way students learn.

Set a time limit for the task and tell them that there will be a share time at the end of the activity.

Painting using one form of Aboriginal art.

courage students
plan first and
cate roles to
up members.

2 Set a specific focus for the students

I would like you to paint a part of the creek that you saw yesterday in which you saw evidence of change.

Build a 'before and after' model showing the way an area of the park might have looked a hundred years ago.

You may offer a variety of forms or media for example:

frieze	paint	dioramas
clay	window painting	construction
posters	silk screen	collage
mobiles	lino cuts	strip sets
potato cuts	photographs	tapestry
charcoal	newsletter	chalk
models	mapping 2D, 3D	

The materials you offer students may depend on their previous art experiences.

(b) DRAMA ACTIVITIES

PURPOSES

(i) To use drama or role play as a means of representing ideas arising from the shared experience.

(ii) To provide students with the opportunity to view situations from the perspective/s of particular groups or individuals.

(iii) To help students understand the impact of changes on the individuals involved.

(iv) To help students explore and clarify their own and other peoples' values.

You will need to make sure that students are clear about the purposes of the activity, for example:

Our task is to dramatise some of the ways we saw people interacting with the environment yesterday. In doing this, we will be exploring and sharing what different people feel about their environment.

Role play

Role play cards or costumes may help with character development.

Present students with a hypothetical problem that involves the area visited or read about (perhaps linked to the class serial). For example, the area may be proposed for development. Allocate roles, e.g. a resident, a conservationist, a town planner, etc. Groups with the same roles meet to discuss and prepare their response to the problem. Hold a mock public meeting to debate the issue. Make some recommendations.

Mime

This can be a powerful way to express experience. Students could develop short scenarios relating to the shared experience (e.g. an incident they observed). They may take on different roles (an animal, ranger, visitor, student) and mime the scene from the various characters' perspectives.

Formal debate

It is very important that students are debriefed after the debate and that they engage in some form of reflection on the experience. Ask students, 'How did you feel? Why?'

This is similar to the role play although here students present their arguments about a hypothetical or real problem in a formal debate. Groups can be divided into those 'for', those 'against', an arbitration group to monitor proceedings, and research groups to help each side with the development of their argument.

News reports

Select a local environmental issue, perhaps related to the site you visited or the video you viewed, preferably one that has been reported in the local newspaper. In groups, students prepare a TV or radio news item about the issue. This should include a report on the issue and interviews with various related characters. News reports are presented in television style or could be taped and made into a radio broadcast.

Documentaries

Videos could be viewed by parents and other classes as one form of action.

Students work in groups to devise short, documentary style presentations to explain something they have learnt through the shared experience. These could be combined with some art and music and filmed on video. *Tell It on Video* (Stow 1989) provides excellent advice on how to do this.

Movement

This could be a joint effort by classroom and specialist teachers.

Students can combine movement, art and music in a performance representing a theme or issue explored during the shared experience.

For example, a movement performance with music and sound effects which portrays the way an area has changed over time.

(c) MATHS ACTIVITIES

PURPOSES
(i)   To use mathematics as a means of organising, representing and interpreting information.
(ii) To use mathematics as a vehicle for the development of thought in the content areas.

Throughout the unit students may gather data about people and the environment. For example, they could work out how much rubbish is thrown away at home or in the classroom each day, week, month or year. They could also find out how many electrical appliances are used in an average day/week, etc. This data could be brought to the class and represented in appropriate ways, such as graphs.

Students may also have gathered data during the shared experience which can be organised and represented graphically, for example:
• types of rubbish in the park
• evidence of animal life along various sections of the creek
• jobs held by people involved in protecting a natural area.

These data may be presented in a variety of ways. Make the purpose of the activity explicit to the students, for example:

How can we present the information which we have gathered about people and the environment so that it can be very easily understood?

Various forms of mathematical representation could be considered, for example:

bar graphs	decimals	line graphs
fractions	picture graphs	percentages
pie graphs	3-dimensional graphs	

You should also consider the use of various media. A range of art materials should be available, together with three-dimensional materials such as Lego, multi-link and MAB blocks. Computers and calculators can help with calculations. Computer spreadsheets and databases also have the capacity to draw graphs using the chart feature.

Encourage students to make generalisations based on their visual representations.

What does your graph tell us about change in this environment?

It may also be appropriate to present students with relevant data about the changing environment and have them compare and interpret statistics used in the resources they have come across during the unit so far. These data could be visually represented in similar ways. Relevant statistical data are available from departments of conservation and environment protection authorities.

aking the
rpose of the
tivity explicit.

udents learn
rough problem
lving.

(d) LANGUAGE ACTIVITIES

> **PURPOSES**
> (i)   To use language to help students to formulate and express concepts and generalisations
> (ii) To allow students to use and share a variety of words, sentence structures and forms of writing which can form the basis of future language activities, such as word study, spelling and syntax.

Writing

Encourage students to write down some of their responses to information gathered, for example:

- personal writing of various kinds
- a language experience book where individuals contribute a page or a small group may decide a particular sequence
- a poem, letter or play

Listing

A 1-3-6 grouping strategy could be used to encourage consensus.

Lists are made individually, then exchanged with a partner, then a small group. For example:

List all the ways that the creek has changed.

List all of the changes to the natural environment that we have observed.

Classification of items on the beach.

Grouping
For example:
   Now I want you to group all the changes that belong together.

Labelling
For example:
   Can you give a name to each of your groups?
Labelling art work done earlier in the unit.

Sharing and challenging
For example:
   Compare your groups with those of your partner or with the rest of your group.
   We can challenge students and encourage them to challenge each other through questions such as:
   What is similar about all of the items in this group?
   Does this term belong here?
   Why do you think it does?

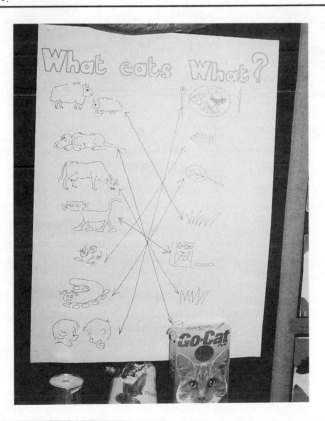

Sharing findings.

(e) STATEMENTS OF GENERALISATION

his can be done
dividually, then
odified by small
oups.

You can now ask students to formulate some statements of generalisation, for example:
   What can we now say about the changing environment?

You may ask groups to generalise about certain aspects of the topic, for example:

What can we say about people and the changing environment?

A generalisation about the needs of living things.

Encourage students to challenge and question statements. This can also be an opportune time to explore the values that lie behind the statements.

These statements can be written:
- as individual statements
- in a language experience book
- as a record of the generalisations of a small group
- on large sheets of paper as a class synthesis

Make sure that these generalisations are kept for future reference as students may want to modify them as their knowledge develops during the unit. It is important that each student is able to find their own statements. These could be kept in folders as part of assessment and evaluation records. Statements made at this stage may be compared with earlier ideas from the tuning in stage. Encourage students to evaluate the changes in their ideas and understandings about the topic.

Compare the students' generalisations with your statements of specific understanding.

Compare the students' generalisations with the specific understandings you listed in the initial planning stage. This allows you to evaluate the degree to which students have developed the ideas you thought important.

(e) CONCEPT MAPS

These could be done using the technique outlined on page 39. This time, the purpose is to show what students have learnt about the topic.

The concept maps from the tuning in stage could be revisited and modified if desired.

48

Triceratops was a plant-eater.

A statement about a dinosaur.

FURTHER READING ACTIVITIES

Cloze

In cloze activities, students provide a suitable word where there has been a deletion from a sentence. They are designed to develop a learner's ability to predict using various reading cues. Some of the statements of generalisation may be useful for cloze activities:

> *Most of the rubbish found in our creek was _____ .*
>
> *If people used _____ rather than _____ they would cause less damage to the environment.*

Values clarification — Specific applications of cloze for the integrated program involve the deletion of words which convey the author's values and attitudes including sexism, racism and other forms of bias. The students' replacements may then be compared with the original and comment invited. Newspaper articles on environmental issues could be analysed in a similar way.

Directed reading/thinking activities

Limit the amount of text. — This reading strategy is designed to help students formulate and test hypotheses based on explicit information and inference from printed text. You need to be able to control the amount of text at any given time through the use of wall sheets, a duplicated story with page breaks in appropriate places, or overhead transparencies.

Students are asked to predict what will happen, then they test and modify these predictions as more text is uncovered. The success of this activity depends on finding material which relates to the shared experience and your understandings and which is unknown to the students.

FURTHER WRITING ACTIVITIES

Reports, explanations, expositions.

Students may now be in a position to use a variety of writing forms in order to publish some of their ideas and interpretations. These could include reports, explanations or expositions, and could take the form of books, newspapers, articles or letters.

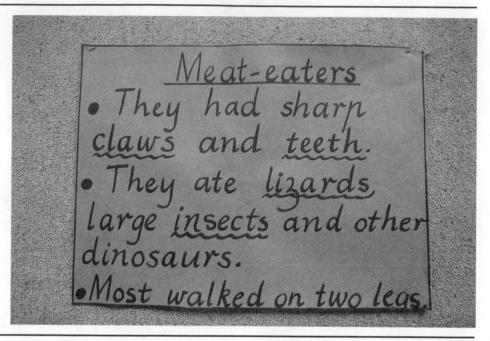

A simple report on meat-eating dinosaurs.

Production of small-group or class books relating to the shared experience and using the picture/story format is a very successful as a 'published' writing activity. Opportunities for writing in a range of genres will present themselves throughout the unit. Students should be exposed to a range of text styles as models.

7 RELATED EXPERIENCES

PURPOSES
(i) To extend the unit (if appropriate) in more specific directions as a result of insights gained from the initial experience.
(ii) To provide more information in order to broaden the range of understandings available to the students.

Related experiences will largely be directed by the nature of the topic, and the outcomes of the shared experience.

(a) FILMS/VIDEOTAPES/PICTURES

These may be of a more instructional nature than the experiential type used in the shared experience. Films dealing with situations which are remote from the learner's direct experience may also be appropriate at this stage. For example, a film dealing with the environment in another country and the different ways people rely on, care for and affect that environment.

(b) A VISIT TO A CONTRASTING SITE
This allows students to investigate a different type of environment or alternative evidence of change.

(c) FURTHER INTERVIEWS TO CLARIFY AND REFINE IDEAS
For examples, students could interview local residents about their opinions of a particular area of the suburbs and ways they believe it has changed or should change.

(d) GAMES
Games that explore basic environmental concepts can help students to refine their understandings. For example, in 'The Webbing Game' students take on the role of different plants, animals and other natural resources and have to show how these things are interrelated by connecting with each other using a ball of string.

(e) READING

Picture story-books
Select picture story-books that:
• portray change in the environment
• explore conservation issues
• encourage children to consider feelings, values and attitudes associated with change.

Sharing a big book.

A display of books used in an integrated unit.

Baker, J. *Window*, Random Century, Sydney, 1991.
Dr Suess, *The Lorax*, Collins, London, 1972.
Morimoto, J. *Kenju's Forest*, William Collins, London, 1989.
Peet, B. *The Wump World*, Deutsch, London, 1970.
Reece, J. *Lester and Clyde*, Ashton Scholastic, Gosford, 1976.
Wheatley, N. *My Place*, Collins Dove, Melbourne, 1987.

Factual texts
Select factual texts that:
• provide additional information to shared experiences
• extend children's understandings of key issues
• provide models for children's writing
Coleridge, A. *Feral Animals*, Macmillan, Melbourne, 1987.
Drew, D. *The Earth in Danger!*, Nelson, Melbourne, 1990.

(f) SIMULATION GAMES
For example, 'Australia 2020', available from the Gould League of
Victoria. In this game students have to make decisions about the future

of the environment. This is a most useful way for them to begin to apply their learning and further refine their understandings.

8 SORTING OUT RELATED EXPERIENCES

Once again, students need opportunities to work through the ideas raised through this new information. Some students may want to modify some of their earlier generalisations.

What can we now say about the changing environment?

DATA CHARTS

Students can complete small-group or whole class data charts which summarise and compare information gathered during the shared and related experiences. An example is given below where change in different environments is compared. This could be done using a computer database and may be an ongoing activity as additional information is gathered. Further generalisations could be drawn from the chart.

We should not unduly pressure students to modify their generalisations, nor is there any point in our trying to obtain consensus on these generalisations at a class level. Students will only modify their generalisations through further experience and increased understanding.

compare these revised generalisations with your specific understandings for evaluation purposes.

PLACE	BRIEF DESCRIPTION	HABITAT FOR	THREATENED BY	CAN BE PROTECTED BY	IF LOST
School yard	buildings, grass areas, bitumen, native trees	insects, birds, (especially sparrows), people	children playing in wrong area, litter	signs, more playing areas	not as nice a place to work in, fewer animals
Park	trees, flower beds, swings	birds, insects, possums, people	bike riding on wrong areas	better paths, park rangers	nowhere to relax and play
Rainforest	heavily reed, dark, damp	many birds and animals	logging	not buying rainforest products	fewer birds and animals, climate change
Wetlands	wet! noisy, reeds, mud	water birds, fish, reptiles	pollution, (e.g. sewage), draining	better waste disposal systems, less chemicals	less fresh water, less bird and animal life

9 REFLECTION AND ACTION

PURPOSES

(i) To empower students and help to develop the belief that they can be effective participants in society.

(ii) To help students to make links between their understandings and their experience in the real world.

(iii) To provide further insight into students' understandings for future unit planning.

When planning an action component, teachers and students need to consider the following:

- whether the action will be designed/carried out by individuals, small groups or the whole class
- the time and resources available
- what the action aims to achieve
- how the effectiveness of the action can be monitored
  There are a number of possible forms of action:
- **Involvement** in some sort of environmental improvement in the school ground or at a local site, e.g. tree planting, weeding, setting up a compost heap.

Students should initiate these tasks individually or in small groups.

- **Letter writing:**
  - to the newspaper
  - to an organisation
  - to a local politician
  - to the school council
  - to local community groups (e.g. shopkeepers) with suggestions or comments relating to the natural environment
- **Publishing** an article for the school newsletter or local newspaper
- **Setting up a campaign** or program within the school community, e.g. recycling or waste reduction
- **Giving talks** to other grades or schools, showing work done in the unit
- **Setting up information displays** at a local community centre (e.g. library, bank), or school entry hall

Students should evaluate the success of their actions.

- **Devising personal action contracts** that will be carried out at home — changing habits or forming new ones
- **Designing and maintaining an area** of the school grounds to encourage native birds and animals to use it as habitat.

EVALUATION

Evaluation procedures and suggestions are throughout the above sequence of activities, reflecting the manner in which we think they are best carried out. Further elaboration of evaluation and assessment strategies is undertaken in chapter 5.

4
LANGUAGE AND
INTEGRATED
LEARNING

David Hornsby and **Jo-ann Parry** show how teachers can relate integrated learning and specific curriculum programs. They have used a language program as their example and demonstrate that integrated learning approaches need not be all encompassing. One of the strengths of the model advocated in this book is its flexibility. It allows teachers to capture the language generated in an integrated learning program and to then use it to develop the necessary skills in an appropriate and meaningful context.

◆

The curriculum model presented in this book identifies specific stages when language is used to process information related to a unit of work. However, language is used through all stages of most learning, not just at these specific times. The language program is in operation the moment the students enter the classroom and it continues all day. Language crosses all subject boundaries. Learners learn about the world through language and, in so doing, they learn language and learn about language (Halliday 1982).

Learners have opportunities to develop their language skills and strategies *all day,* and the teacher may organise the program so that these opportunities are maximised. However, teachers may have different times during the day when they focus on helping learners with particular skills, understandings, concepts and behaviours related to specific subject areas. For example, during the morning 'language workshop', students may be reading or writing materials that have arisen from the integrated unit in progress. The teacher will be focusing on helping the students to learn *about* language. In an afternoon session, the students may again be reading and writing materials that are related to the unit in progress, but the teacher is now focusing on helping the students with concepts and understandings being developed through the content of the unit (with the emphasis on learning *through* language).

The teacher therefore has two clear purposes: one which focuses on English language learning (learning language and learning about language) and one which focuses on content learning (learning through language and learning language). These distinctions are not clear cut; there are obviously many overlaps. During the language workshop, the teacher is focusing on what was traditionally called 'English'. During integrated studies, the teacher is focusing on what was traditionally called social education, science or health.

GENERATING LANGUAGE

The core of any language program is the language generated by the students themselves. This language is generated as they interact with others and with resources and materials. The 'others' may include the teacher, peers, classroom visitors, parents and grandparents. The materials may be commercially available, such as picture books, short stories, novels, anthologies of poetry and extracts from literature, audio and video tapes, scripts, non-fiction reference books, and any other 'authentic text'. The materials may also include non-commercial materials: those produced by the students themselves, train timetables, advertising materials, the school newsletter, and so on.

The language of the textbooks, reference books, fiction and a variety of other materials is important, but it is the **processing of language in use** as learners learn together that is mainly responsible for each individual's language development.

MATERIALS AND THE GENERATION OF LANGUAGE

The materials used will influence both the quality and the quantity of the language generated by the learners. Consequently, teachers *do* need to consider carefully the materials that they and the learners will use in the classroom. Sometimes the materials will be provided for prescribed use, sometimes they will be actively sought by the learner who is seeking something specific, and sometimes they will be selected (even casually or randomly) from a wide range available.

The following points should be considered:
- There should be a range of materials with content that supports the unit. Some will reinforce what the learners know; others will challenge and take them beyond their present knowledge.
- Materials should present the designated content in different ways. For example, in some units, all the following forms could be used: picture story books, informational narrative, procedural texts, reports, poetry, video, film, filmstrips, picture sets.
- Previous materials used by the learners should be considered. If, for example, informational narrative materials were available and used in a previous unit of work, the teacher may purposely introduce or emphasise different forms in the current unit.
- A range of readability levels should be provided. There should be

a full range of texts which are simpler, providing support for the reader, and others which are more difficult because they have more challenges. Remember, it is not just the amount of text or the 'difficulty of the words' that make reading materials difficult. It may be the lack of familiarity with the genre. For example, if students have not experienced science report text structure, then it could be very difficult text even though the vocabulary used is simple and known.

- There should be materials which can be revisited for different purposes. For example, a particular book may be used for tuning in to an integrated unit, but may be revisited during language workshops in following weeks in order to study genre, practise audience reading skills, and even to practise specific skills such as finding and listing alternative spellings for the /æ/ sound, finding compound words or building a 'word tree' based on a base word from the text. Revisiting text in this way is guided by the teacher's goals for language learning. These are often written during the initial planning for the whole unit but are also determined (discovered) during the progress of the unit. Students may also choose to go back to the same text for different purposes.

EXPERIENCE AND THE GENERATION OF LANGUAGE

The texts, including aural and visual materials used in the classroom, have a direct impact on the quality and quantity of the language that is generated. However, language is also generated as a result of first-hand experience. These experiences may be spontaneous, planned, individual or shared. Many of the spontaneous and individual experiences are beyond the teacher's control, and need to be! They add to the richness and variety of the language in the classroom. Some unplanned or spontaneous experiences occur in the classroom and, when they are shared by a group or the whole class, they can stimulate interactions that generate an abundance of language.

However, it is also important for **planned,** shared experiences to occur so that shared language is used and developed as learners interact. This shared language provides the teacher with further opportunities to focus on language development as learners:

- prepare for the experience
- share the experience
- process the experience.

This doesn't mean that every shared experience has to be a focus for shared language development. Language will always be involved, but what the teacher and learners do with it will depend on purposes at the time. Not all language generated is used for language teaching! The teacher will be constantly evaluating the needs of the learners and making informed decisions about when to support the challenge, when to stand back and observe, and when to evaluate.

The language generated as a result of the planned shared experiences in the integrated unit will often be used in language workshops. The language planning for the unit 'The Changing Environment' (pp. 64–9) identifies, in the right hand column, opportunities for using the language generated by the students and the language (text) provided in the materials or resources.

When the language *generated* through shared experience is used later in language workshops, the emphasis changes to *shaping* that language.

SHAPING LANGUAGE

When planning a language program, teachers are able to draw upon several 'sources'. For a balanced program, language should be drawn from at least the following three sources:

1 Aspects of language drawn from a current integrated unit of work that they will use and develop during specific language workshops;
2 Aspects of language that attend to the identified needs of the learners (identified whenever language is being used throughout the day);
3 Aspects of language which arises spontaneously from the learners.

To achieve balance and continuity, teachers need to provide structure and regular routines. These can be built into a model for daily language sessions similar to the following:

INTRODUCTORY ACTIVITY
Whole-class teacher planned activity.

QUIET TIME
Includes silent reading, reflective writing (teacher also).

WORKSHOP
An active time in which different groups and individuals are doing different things. Small group work will be a feature. For example, there may be reading/writing conferences and teaching groups. Students will also be free to pursue individual reading/writing tasks (these could include continued silent reading or writing, revising, editing, responses to reading, journal entries, publishing tasks).

SHARE TIME
The whole class comes together again and students have the opportunity to share with others what they have been reading or writing.

This basic structure for language sessions is described in detail in *Write On: A Conference Approach to Writing* (Parry & Hornsby 1985) and *Read On: A Conference Approach to Reading* (Hornsby, Sukarna & Parry 1986). Readers may also wish to refer to *Inside Whole Language: A Classroom View* (Brown & Mathie 1990).

Once an integrated unit is planned and underway, the teacher will seize opportunities for language learning as they arise. For example, *Storm Boy* (Colin Thiele) could be used as a tuning in activity for the unit but valuable language learning can also be developed. Colin Thiele's work lends itself well to an author study. It could be 'revisited' later, in order to study sentence beginnings and to discuss sentence structure. This is deliberate planning to focus students' attention on learning about language.

Planning should incorporate different ways of using the integrated unit to extend students' knowledge and use of language in a variety of contexts. The integrated unit is not only a valuable starting point for language learning; it usually also leads to exploration of language beyond the unit.

The ideas from integrated units (social education, science and technology, environmental education and personal development) also provide some of the substance of the language program. There will be various forms of text, including literature, related to these ideas. Other literature being used in the classroom also provides some of the information for the language program.

ACHIEVING BALANCE IN A LANGUAGE PROGRAM

To achieve a balance, we need to attend to:
- the language that is generated by learners as they encounter and engage with the content of the unit and the texts related to that content
- other texts (not related to the unit content) being shared in the classroom
- the language that is learned and practised as learners engage with reading and writing processes across all areas of the curriculum.

There has sometimes been a misunderstanding that integrated learning means that all the language *must* fit within or come from the content of the topic or unit. Obviously, this is not so. Links between areas of the curriculum are made only when they are natural and when they are related to the understandings on which the unit is focused. The links are not contrived or forced. Activities are not chosen for their own sake. They are chosen because they offer the possibility for the learners to further develop their ideas about the fields of knowledge being studied.

LANGUAGE GOALS

In chapter 3, ideas for planning an integrated unit were illustrated using the topic 'The Changing Environment'. The following understandings were listed for this topic:

- The natural environment is constantly changing.
- There are a range of factors which influence this change.
- Human beings have had an adverse impact on the natural environment.
- People and other animals depend on the natural environment for their survival.
- There are many things that we can do as individuals that will help reduce the stresses on the environment.
- People respond to the changing environment in different ways, but change ultimately affects us all.

These understandings provide a focus for the **content** of the unit. It is also necessary to determine the goals related to the language work to be covered. The content of the unit, and the level for which it is planned (Years 3 and 4), will obviously dictate, to a large extent, the language goals that are set. It is essential for teachers to have these language goals planned and written down before beginning the unit as they provide a focus for the language teaching that occurs throughout the unit, although during planning, and during the implementation of the unit, the initial goals may be adapted and new goals added. If teachers do not know what the intended goals are before the unit starts, their teaching is reduced to 'activity for the sake of activity'. It will lack direction and purpose.

LANGUAGE GOALS FOR THE CHANGING ENVIRONMENT

1 To express and communicate ideas about personal experiences of the environment.
2 To use oral language to organise and share developing ideas about the environment.
3 To become familar with the text structure of the report genre by reading and comparing several reports (include current, local newspaper reports).
4 To use statements of generalisation reached during the unit to jointly construct a class report.
5 To have individual students write their own reports.
6 To use oral language to develop appropriate ways of discussing what learners know and how people use language for a variety of social purposes.
7 To read different texts about the environment and to compare the different forms of writing and text organisation.
8 To generate a list of vocabulary used by the different authors to help them describe the environment (adjectives and adjectival phrases).
9 To complete an author study (Colin Thiele).
10 To enjoy a selection of picture story books that illustrate aspects of the unit.
11 To compare the poetic language used by different authors (e.g. Bill Peet and Kath Walker) to describe the environment.

Once language goals such as these are planned, teachers have direction and a sense of purpose for the language program. The unit

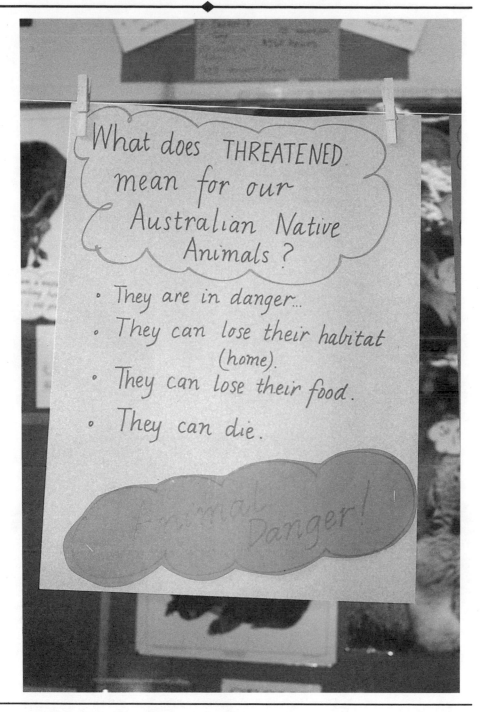

Exploring word meanings.

planner provided on the following pages is a sample of the kind of documentation appropriate for planning purposes. Further plans are also provided to show, in more detail, how language is developed through an integrated unit. The detail shows the relationship between the language program and the integrated unit.

UNIT Our local park **CLASS** 3/4 **4 WEEKS** (___/___/___)

Understandings: (i) The natural environment is constantly changing. (ii) There are a range of factors which influence this change. (iii) Humans have had an adverse impact on the natural environment.

CONTENT Social studies, science and technology, personal development

<table>
<tr><td rowspan="1">TUNING IN</td><td>

Engaging Children

Outdoor activity: children listen to and describe outdoor sounds
Read a page from *Storm Boy* which describes the environment; imagine that you are there; describe what you see and hear. Children share descriptive passages from other texts.

Preparing to find out

Focus questions: Why do we have local parks? What do you know about our local park? Groups paint murals to show the park in the four seasons. Interview parents about their use of the park. List questions for the ranger. Decide on personal issue for study. What animals do you think live in the park? How do you think they affect the park?

</td></tr>
<tr><td>INVESTIGATING</td><td>

Shared experiences — at the local park

1. Session with the ranger
2. Look at leaf and bark samples, make rubbings
3. List types of litter
4. Write information found on any signs
5. List play equipment and facilities
6. Record evidence of animal habitation
7. Record evidence of effects of people
8. Interview people about their use of the park

Gathering, sorting and presenting

Return to work done before the excursion. What do you need to change or add? Take leaf and bark rubbings, sort and label display. What have you found out about people in the park? Animals in the park? Uses and abuses of the park?
Proposal to build a skateboarding ramp in the park — children take roles of various people involved and act out meeting. Writing of argument presenting different points of view and stating conclusion. Writing of draft statements of generalisation in groups — groups meet and whole class statements are prepared. Share further literature, collect newspaper articles.
Revising generalisations.

</td></tr>
<tr><td>OUTCOMES</td><td>

Drawing conclusions, reflection and action

Revising generalisations: What do we know now?
Review statements, photographs, artwork, graphs. Complete a fact sheet (for others) with important, amazing new information.
Planting of seedlings, making a new garden bed, constructions of flower boxes of preparing pot plants. Produce a pamphlet to advertise local park facilities — could involve local council or local newspaper. Design a board game using uses and abuses of the park as 'positives' and 'negatives'.

</td></tr>
</table>

Figure 4.1:
Unit planner

◆

(iv) Animals and people depend on the natural environment for their survival. (v) There are many things that we can do as individuals that will help reduce the stresses on the environment. (vi) People respond to the changing environment in different ways, but change ultimately affects us all.

PROCESSING INFORMATION	RELATED SKILLS AND STRATEGIES	EVALUATION
Language/drama/art/ maths/music	**Activities that emanate from work-in-progress**	**Student assessment**
Oral reading: sharing of ——▶ passages from narratives which describe different environments	skimming and scanning to locate approriate passages.	• Unit booklet: 2 entries per week 1. Content — what have I learned? 2. Process — how did I learn it?
Storytelling: sharing stories about experiences in parks		• Each student to keep a log (or to document in some way) ways in which they gather information (e.g. sketch book, journal, photograph album)
Painting: visual —————▶ representation of knowledge about parks	use of appropriate colours and textures to represent the different seasons	
Interviewing/brainstorming: ——▶ to collect information. Listening to and questioning the ranger. Investigating and recording	writing and asking effective questions	• Reading — a negotiated response to a text by Colin Thiele
Photography		• Writing — a written (and published) report on some aspcet of the unit
Art: leaf and bark rubbings ——▶	image reproduction — a form of printing	• Maths — a completed graph (which is 'published' — shared/explained)
Maths: pattern work — symmetry, tessellations		**Unit evaluation**
Writing: labelling ——————▶	adjectives (describing)	Revisit unit understandings. Were these achieved? Any new (or unplanned) understandings?
Drama: clarification of roles through discussion, role play through meeting. Groups write argumentative ——▶ piece together	summarising skills debating skills in argument presentation statement of position, with accompanying evidence; summary of position	Compare children's generalisations with stated understandings.

Maths: what are the major ——▶ uses of the park (a) people (b) animals? How many types of animals have the park as a habitat? Design a 'key' that indicates habitat (e.g. type, location)	graphing: bar
	          column
	          pie	

Writing/reading: to clarify ——▶ meaning, to find out about procedures	synthesising information from many sources	

PLANNING LANGUAGE FOR THE UNIT

Language highlights

TUNING IN

- Outdoor activity: students listen to and describe outdoor sounds.

- Read *Storm Boy;* discuss (passage on the environment). Visualisation: *Imagine that you are in that environment. Describe what you see and what you hear.*

Listening to describe

Reading to students; **listening** for details; **listening** to build up visual image; **talking** to describe
Author study: Colin Thiele introduced by *Storm Boy;* other titles to be used during language workshops

PREPARING FOR THE SHARED EXPERIENCE

- Preparing students for a visit to a local park. Two focus questions:
  (1) *Why do we have local parks?*
  (2) *What do you know about our local park?*

Oral language: small group brainstorming
Writing: listing from brainstorming

- Four groups to paint murals of the local park at different times of the year (representing the four seasons).

- *Interview your parents about their use of the local park. How is use affected by seasonal change?*

Oral language: interviewing

- *Write to your local ranger to confirm arrangements for the excursion.*

Writing: letter writing. Conventions of formal letter writing

- *What do you want to find out about the local park? How do you think people may affect the park?* This activity should lead to a class list of questions that the students want to ask the ranger when they visit the park, and/or questions to ask people they may meet and interview in the park.

Oral language: raising and discussing questions
Writing: shared writing of list of questions

- Individual students are asked to consider one personal issue that they will pursue further while at the local park. Each student is to record how they intend to gather the information they require (this could be in writing, in photographs, in sketches or diagrams or maps, etc.)

Writing: recording intentions

- *What animals do you think live in the park? How do you think they may affect the park?* Students: (a) brainstorm from own knowledge; (b) browse through information sheets and pamphlets obtained from local councils and government or semigovernment bodies.

Oral language: small group or whole class brainstorming
Reading: for specific information; sharing of information

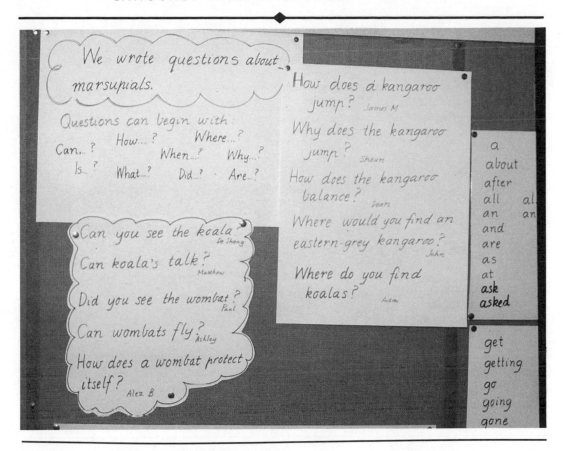

Focusing on conventions associated with questions.

THE SHARED EXPERIENCE

Groups are arranged so that only one group at a time is with the ranger. Others are responsible for completing the following activities:

- gather leaf and bark samples; do rubbings and sketches and then return the samples

- list types of litter found in the park

- write down the information found on any signs in the park

- list the various types of play equipment and other facilities provided.

- look for evidence of animal habitation and to record in appropriate ways

- look for evidence of effects that people have had on the park

- interview people in the park about their use of the park

Language highlights

Oral language: listening to and questioning the ranger

Oral and written language: to discuss, investigate and record

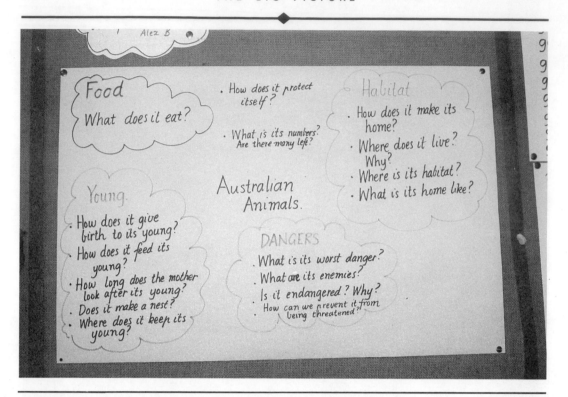

Concepts about Australian animals.

Writing about rainforests.

PROCESSING THE SHARED EXPERIENCE

The students now need opportunities to sort the information that has been gathered. They could:

- return to the drawings and murals completed before the excursion. What might they need to add or change as a result of the visit to the park? After making necessary changes, prepare to share with the rest of the class.

- sort leaf and bark rubbings; display and label.

- from their notes, see what they have found out about:
  - people in the park
  - animals in the park
  - uses (or abuses) of the park

Students should prepare information so that it can be presented to the whole class.

- Individuals or pairs determine an area or an issue that they wish to investigate further.

A group of residents has written to the local council requesting permission to build a skateboarding ramp in an area of the park. At the meeting, the following people will be presenting their cases:
1 Home owner who lives next door to the park
2 The ranger (chairperson)
3 The local skateboarding champion
4 A local youth worker
5 The president of the local bird-watching club
6 Owner of the fast-food outlet across the road
7 A gardener for the local council

- Number the students from 1 to 7 to assign roles as listed above. Students wear labels to show their role.

- All students with the same role meet to clarify the role they will play in the meeting. Rangers are reminded that they will be chairing any meetings and will eventually be required to pass on recommendations to the local council.

- Students jot down the arguments they would use to support their views.

- Students are then free to lobby others in the classroom. (They may decide not to do this in order to keep their arguments for the meeting when they may have more impact.)

- Hold the meetings with the rangers in the chair.

Joint text construction. Argument presenting both points of view and stating some conclusion.

Language highlights

Oral language: presentation of class: focus on presentation skills

Writing: labelling

Writing/reading: summarising; synthesising; writing of related information into paragraphs; publishing decisions

Drama/oral language: clarification of roles through discussion

Writing: reminder notes; summarising

Oral language: using persuasive language to convince others; express opinion; present point of view with supporting reasons; justify judgements made; distinguish between fact and opinion

• Whole class comes together. Students have had opportunities to hear points of view as a result of the dramatised meeting. All students now contribute to a whole class listing of points for and against. The teacher takes notes on the chalkboard.

STATEMENTS OF GENERALISATION
The students are now asked to formulate some statements of generalisation.

• Groups of four students are asked to generalise about certain aspects of the topic. They may be helped by questions such as:
  • What can we now say about the changing environment?
  • How do people affect the environment?
  • What else affects the environment?
  • How do we depend upon the environment?
  • How do people protect the environment?

• Groups write draft statements of generalisations; agreed statements written on sentence strips for sharing.

• Whole class meets together to share statements of generalisation. They are 'collapsed' into whole class statements and written on charts.

RELATED EXPERIENCES
Select from the following activities those which will further develop the unit understandings. Negotiate this according to your assessment of students' needs and interests. The decision will be further influenced by the work being covered in concurrent language workshops.

Literature
Select a range of literature which allows students to explore ideas related to the unit. These ideas may have emerged during the shared experience or may reflect individual or group interests. The following list of books represents a small sample of literature appropriate to a unit on *The Changing Environment: Our Local Park.*

Millicent (Jeannie Baker) — Use Post-it labels stating what people are doing in the park

Nikki's Walk (Jane Tanner) — non-text book about neighbourhood

Language highlights
Writing: joint construction of an argumentative text with statement of points of evidence and summary of position.

Oral language: discussion

Writing: drafting initial statements; revising; editing (punctuation, sentence structure, grammar, spelling, handwriting)

Group writing: groups reach consensus and write statements

Reading: summarising the main points.

Reading: author study on Colin Thiele continues

Writing: labelling

Oral language: composing own oral text

Newspapers
Students find any article on the natural environment and bring for class scrap book. Add article with comments.

Over time, students read about a particular environmental issue in their local area. Develop a point of view, discuss with others; write to the local newspaper.

Earth Watch (TV)
Tape a few *Earth Watch* segments. Groups script their own *Earth Watch* segments.

Maps and graphic information
Obtain maps and aerial photographs for students to compare country areas, inner suburban parks, sports fields, botanic gardens, etc.

REVISING GENERALISATIONS
The earlier generalisations are now considered in the light of new information gained through the related activities.

Earlier statements are modified if necessary.

REFLECTION AND ACTION
• The students are involved in different forms of environmental action, such as planting trees or shrubs in the park visited earlier and in the school grounds.

• The writing of a fact sheet to go home to the school community (including parents, shopkeepers, nearby residents). This could include household hints, reasons to compost, ways of reducing rubbish, care of community parks and gardens, etc.

• Local newspaper. The local paper may be prepared to publish the fact sheet.

Language highlights

Reading: scanning and selecting relevant materials
Writing: commentaries
Reading: for information to develop a point of view
Writing: a letter to express your point of view

Reading: intrepreting visual text about issues beyond the local environment
Writing: scriptwriting

Reading: specific skills of map and photograph reading

Reading: of earlier statements
Oral language: discussion
Writing: revising and writing new generalisations

Reading: procedural text (planting trees) or other relevant material

Writing: various forms of text (procedural, factual, recount); layout (text, graphics); publication issues

MANAGING TIME TO ALLOW FOR EFFECTIVE LEARNING

The timetable on p. 71 sets out one way of using time effectively. Some variations may be necessary depending on timetabling practicalities and the common use of specialist teachers for areas such as art and library, and a few curriculum activities (such as sport) may require changes on a particular day.

Many schools prevent significant blocks of time for learning by the way in which they cut up the daily timetable. We believe that the fragmented timetable causes fragmented learning styles and frustration.

Many students never experience engagement in significant learning for extended periods of time. Just as they become involved in an activity, the fragmented timetable requires them to change in mid-stream.

In the daily timetable suggested, more substantial blocks of time are available for engagement in more significant learning. Any one-hour block of time may be swapped with another; however, areas of curriculum which have been traditionally separated may be built in to the integrated unit even though they are taken by specialist teachers. For example, a library session **is** one of the one-hour blocks of time for communication and/or investigation. If students are involved in an integrated unit on transport, a session in the art room may see them designing future forms of transport and making 3-D models (the art teacher will still help students with specific skills, strategies, understandings and attitudes related to art).

STUDENT FOCUS

The focus for students during every block of time is **learning.** At times, they will be required by the teacher for specific things (e.g. teaching groups, conferences, assessment). At other times, they will be responsible for making their own decisions about what needs to be done and the timetable shows some of the alternatives.

TEACHER FOCUS

'Focus' does not mean 'attend exclusively to', but if a teacher does not have set times for focusing on particular skills, strategies, understandings, behaviours and attitudes, then many important things can end up being integrated out of existence. (This happened to spelling in many early writing classrooms.) Also, if a teacher has a routine, the students know what kind of help they can expect and when they can expect it.

ROUTINES AND EXPECTATIONS

*The best classrooms we've seen are those where **routines** and **expectations** are clear and understood by all.*

With an integrated curriculum, there is more need than ever before for very definite structures and a very clear sense of direction. Teaching/learning will only have this sense of direction, will only be purposeful, when integrated unit understandings and language goals are clearly identified, documented and used as the basis for planning. They may be modified and other understandings and goals may be added during the course of the unit, but it is the prior planning that sets the scene.

The left-hand 'teacher' column of the timetable shows that it is the **teacher's** time which is more structured. From, say 9:00 to 10:00 am,

TEACHER	STUDENTS
Focus: **Communication/English langauge**	**Focus:** **Learning**
9:00 Teacher focuses on helping students with READING skills, strategeis, understandings, behaviours and attitudes. 10:00 Teacher focuses on helping students with WRITING skills, strategies, understandings, behaviours and attitudes.	Students READ self-selected texts related to the integrated unit, texts related to their own enquiries and/or WRITE their own texts related to the integrated unit being studied. Will include dramatic and artistic expression.
11:00 Morning recess	
Focus: **Investigation/maths**	**Focus:** **Learning**
11:20 Teacher focuses on helping students with MATHS skills, strategies, understandings, behaviours and attitudes.	Students involved in inquiry related to MATHS learning and/or maths related to or generated by the integrated unit. Will include reading/writing 'of and for' maths. May include dramatic and artistic expression.
Focus: Investigation/communication expression **Integrated unit** (Content from social education, science, environmental education, personal development)	**Focus:** **Learning**
1:15 Teacher focuses in helping students with the inquiry process and with the development of concepts and generalisations related to social education, science and technology, environmental education, personal development. 3.30	Students involved in inquiry: • tuning in activities • collecting and sorting data • presenting data • outcomes (reporting, social action, etc.) Includes reading/writing related to the inquiry; dramatic, musical and artistic express.

Figure 4.2: A timetable to allow for effective learning. Includes an afternoon recess break from 2:15 - 2:25

the teacher's main efforts will be directed toward helping students with *reading* skills, strategies, understandings, behaviours and attitudes. When the teacher follows the same basic daily routine, students can predict what the teacher is going to do next. They know that they can rely on getting help with reading during this time; that this time of the day will include a reading conference and a teaching group they may be required to attend, or free to attend if they wish. They know that if they want help with a mathematics problem, it is generally more appropriate to wait until the session from 11:20 to 12:20 when the teacher will be focusing on helping students with mathematics skills, strategies, understandings, behaviours and attitudes.

As noted 'focusing' does not mean 'attending exclusively to'; the teacher may be focusing on maths at this time, but obviously, he or she may also be helping students *write* up the mathematics understandings they have developed. There will be attention, therefore, to the appropriate genre for this type of writing. This is the nature of integrated teaching/learning.

5

ASSESSMENT AND EVALUATION

Jeni Wilson looks closely at evaluation and assessment from the perspectives of the learner, the teacher and the school community. She examines the way in which an integrated learning approach requires comprehensive and systematic observation, analysis and record-keeping procedures. She uses several classroom examples which show how children can take greater responsibility for their own progress and achievement, and includes many practical suggestions for teachers to implement in their own classrooms.

◆

An integrated approach to teaching and learning caters for individual differences in learning outcomes. Throughout a unit, students may be expressing their knowledge of a topic through art, drama, oral language, mathematics and a variety of written language forms. We need, therefore, similar diversity in our evaluation and assessment procedures. The strategies outlined in this chapter reflect this diversity and provide opportunities to assess several aspects of learning and teaching which characterise this approach.

When undertaking any form of assessment, we need to have a clear picture of its purposes and an awareness of how our assessment procedures add to the general evaluation of our classroom program and organisation.

DEVELOPING A CLEAR PICTURE

Assessment and evaluation are integral parts of the educational process and all aspects of teaching and learning provide opportunities for both. Assessment is the process of collecting and analysing information about performance. Assessment should reflect the curriculum and its goals, which determine what is to be assessed and how it is to be assessed. Evaluation makes use of this information to make informed decisions about future programs, activities and organisation. Evaluation therefore depends on assessment. Teaching objectives and evaluation are naturally linked together; one cannot function effectively or purposefully without the other.

EIGHT WAYS TO GET VALUE FROM ASSESSMENT

1 Make assessment an integral part of your teaching.
2 Use a variety of techniques (selection should be determined by the purpose of the activities).
3 Ensure that your assessment strategies are easily understood by students.
4 Be positive, by assessing what students know and the progress they have made.
5 Assess a broad range of skills and processes, for example, thinking processes, co-operative group skills, etc.
6 Assess not only what students know, but also how they think and feel about their learning.
7 Collect information continually, filing notes and work samples. Initial understandings or predictions can be filed and compared with later generalisations.
8 Use data collected to make program decisions.·

ASSESSING WHAT STUDENTS DO

ASSESSING WHAT STUDENTS LEARN

Integrated learning is driven by content: by planned strategies which allow students to extend and refine their knowledge of the world. Therefore, planned understandings relating to various topics in the content subjects will be the driving force for assessing what the students already know and what they might learn as a result of their participation in the units. By keeping students' initial generalisations and comparing these with statements generated later in the unit, we can assess what students have learnt about the content of the topic. Here are some examples of statements made by Year 6 students at Eltham East Primary School on a topic about the settlement of Melbourne:

* Melbourne got more civilised during the last 100 years.
* Melbourne started getting polluted around the 1900s.
* The Yarra decreased in size when people started building in Melbourne.

THINGS TO DO
* Ask students to write down three things they have learnt about the topic at various stages throughout the unit.
* Use the 1-3-6 consensus strategy to reduce the number of statements to form a class list. Students individually list a nominated number of statements (say two) about a topic. They then form groups of three to pool ideas, selecting three statements to represent the group. Each group of three then joins another to form a group of six to choose or refine a specific number of statements.

ASSESSING WHAT IS IMPORTANT

Students' levels of participation and engagement in activities and the ways in which they demonstrate what they are learning will also be a focus for assessment. The effectiveness of the teaching strategies and the selection and use of resources can be reconsidered in the light of students' learning behaviour and the learning outcomes.

In an integrated learning environment, opportunities to assess are rich and many. Interactive assessment is possible in this approach because group work and active participation free us at times to rove and mingle with the learners.

Assessment does not have to be written. There are opportunities during independent working time to discuss with students what they are doing, how they feel and the progress they are making. Questioning and feedback are vitally important for student learning and for the teacher in the assessment process. Verbal feedback has the advantage of being immediate and it enables the student to have input:

> *It is through our assessment that we communicate to our pupils those things that we most value. We have an obligation to students to ensure that our assessment contributes to the learning of our pupils and that all those skills and attributes which we most wish to foster receive the recognition of the appropriate assessment. (Clark 1988, Preface)*

Clark's statement has profound implications for classroom practice. For instance, it means that if we value co-operative group skills we must take time to assess them. If we believe reflection is an important part of the learning and assessment process we must allow time for it. Furthermore, we must make it explicit to students why we think these things are important. Assessment and learning objectives should be made clear to students throughout the unit.

A variety of appropriate strategies is the best way to accumulate information about the progress of your students and the effectiveness of your program. As well as providing clear directions for future planning, assessment should enhance motivation and provide starting points for further learning. A number of strategies are outlined in this chapter. Selection should be based on the activities, experiences and the planned understandings appropriate to the unit.

The major task is to develop systematic ways of observing and recording student progress. Aspects of student progress include:

- increasing understanding of ideas and concepts
- developing confidence and independence
- developing co-operative group skills
- reflecting on what has been learned
- demonstrating the ability to self-assess
- developing inquiry and research skills

NEGOTIATED LEARNING AND SELF-ASSESSMENT

The kids were my greatest teachers . . . Whenever I responded to their genuine interests, it worked. If I tried to insert something artificial, it died.

Assessment becomes more meaningful to students if they are involved in the planning and evaluation of integrated curriculum units. We also show that we value their contributions. Although teachers normally decide on the overall unit and understandings (what they want the students to learn), students can negotiate various aspects. For example, students can decide what they want to find out about, how they will investigate it, with whom they will work, and how they will present their findings. Some teachers involve students in planning excursions and listing questions they want answered. This emphasis on student decision-making has influenced how we view and define curriculum.

The curriculum is no longer a prepackaged course to be taken; it is a jointly enacted composition that grows and changes as it proceeds. A new definition of curriculum is needed and new ways of evaluating it must be found (Boomer 1982, p. 150)

Students can also be encouraged to reflect on the process of refining their knowledge of a topic (either mentally, orally or in written form). The following questions may help:
• What did we find out?
• Did we answer our questions?
• Did we find and answer other questions?
• What methods did we use? Were they appropriate/helpful?
• What did we do well?
• What could we improve?
• What do we still need to do?
For these reflections to be valuable the student (and teacher) must be clear about their goals and what is required to meet those goals.

THINGS TO DO
• Involve students in brainstorming appropriate assessment processes.
• After each session, ask students questions such as, What did you learn? What questions do you now have? How can we answer these questions? (These can be done individually, in a small group or as a whole group activity. Responses can be either oral or written).
• If you prefer written self-assessments, structured but open-ended, the following format may be helpful:

LEARNING REPORT

Name/s: _____

Topic: _____

What I/we did: _____

_____

What I/we used to help me/us: _____

_____

What I/we learnt: _____

_____

What I/we still want to find about: _____

_____

Other comments: _____

_____

WHY BOTHER WITH SELF/PEER ASSESSMENT?

Self-assessment does take time, but it has undeniable benefits — it can reveal information that other strategies may never reveal. As teachers we cannot know the struggles and the extra work put into all tasks. The people who really know are the ones who did the work — the students. They are the experts on themselves. Students generally assess themselves accurately. They are more likely to be harsher in judging their own performance than the teacher.

Apart from being non-competitive and non-comparative, self-assessment strategies show students that we value their opinions. They encourage reflection and give students greater responsibility for their own learning. Assessment of oneself has more meaning and impact than the same assessment from a teacher.

Mathematics e.g. Counting, Place Value, Fractions, Processes, Measurement, Problem Solving

> I like times tables. I just have to learn my 13's and 14's better I'm not to good at fractions. I know place value and + ÷ x − and all those I have to learn.

Troy (8 years)

SELF-ASSESSMENT USING JOURNALS

Another strategy is to have students keep journals in which they are asked to describe what they have learnt, to ask questions, state hypotheses, make predictions and organise information. They can also include how they felt about what they learnt, what helped/hindered their learning and any further action required. Comments or questions from teachers can be added to these journals, establishing a written dialogue and showing that what students say is valued:

> *Sometimes we ignore one of the most important sources of diagnostic information — students' perceptions of their own achievements. Teachers can be helped in the development of goals by talking to students about the stage they believe they are at, and comparing this to where students themselves believe they are at. (Ministry of Education, Victoria 1988b, p.69)*

Social sciences e.g. Social Education, Science, Health Education,

> I learnt all about the envourvent and all the kinds of chemicals that effect the OZONE LAYER

SYSTEMATIC OBSERVATION AND ANECDOTAL NOTES

Due to their apparent lack of structure, informal assessment strategies such as anecdotal records or kidwatching are sometimes not recognised as being important and informative. Some people believe that informal assessment is subjective and inaccurate but, by using carefully thought out criteria which matches your objectives, kidwatching can be as rigorous as traditional forms of assessment. In contrast, test results have often just confirmed teachers' beliefs about students' competencies and weaknesses, and offer no new useful information. Test items rarely give us good information about the perceptions and insights of our students.

Name these shapes

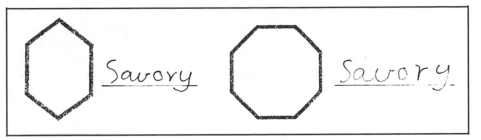

How would you evaluate this response? An incorrect answer or a student making links between a test item and her/his life experience?

Anecdotal notes are really just teachers' jottings of observed significant events which could include work, behaviour, interactions, etc. Accurate descriptive accounts of individuals supplemented with other assessment data, such as interviews, questionnaires and self-assessment, form a broad and powerful description of particular classroom events.

> Hannah Rose
> 2/2 quiet but a contributor in cooperative group.
> 10/2 planned work using a concept map
> 22/2 changes made to concept map show understanding of the concept
> 8/3 chosen as reporter — spoke clearly — able to justify decisions
> 19/3 Brought a book to share with class.

THINGS TO DO

- Next time your students are working independently, make some jottings. Decide what to focus on, for example, a specific behaviour or ability, a selected number of students, or evidence of a growing understanding:

UNDERSTANDING: EVERYONE IS DIFFERENT

Students talked freely about their skills and weaknesses. Skye said she needs to work on her handwriting. She quoted her mother: 'You can't be good at everything.' Students amazed me during the tuning in activity. They had a better understanding of and empathy towards people with disabilities than I had expected. Will ask students for their words to form concept maps instead of using mine. May need to consider a larger range of more sophisticated resources.

WAYS OF RECORDING

By keeping informal notes of students' progress, we can make sure that significant information is not forgotten. One easy way is to have a class list on a clipboard. This method helps us keep tabs on all students. Lists of conferences, teaching groups, share time participants, etc., can be kept together on the clipboard as well.

Some teachers like to keep their own journal of the day's/week's events. This can also include comments about the way students responded to certain activities, the resources used, different grouping strategies, etc. Whatever system is used to keep anecdotal notes, it must be easily accessible, quick and simple.

WEEK: 8

	COMMENTS	FOLLOW UP
Bavulovski, Georgea.	(+Tania) brainstormed ideas for topic. enthusiastic "shower"	✓
Camenzuli, Danny.	voice projection ✓	
Dalakis, Tania	(See Georgea) contributing in group	
Dunn, Kristy,	details in drawings, ready to share	
Hart, Mathew,	Researched at library (self motivated)	

Reminders

* Teaching Group – concept mapping
    Leanne, Sean, Leanne, Danny

CHECKLISTS

Checklists provide a quick overview of a student's performance and can be used as indicators of growth and progress (cognitive and social). They can also be used as a guide for future observations by providing a reminder of behaviour/skills/understandings to watch for.

Example: Are students developing understandings, confidence, independence, co-operative group skills and the ability to reflect on their own progress?

Checklists are more appropriate when developed by the teacher during unit planning, so that they reflect the planned understandings for the unit. We need to ensure that they are suited to the particular group of students. Students can be involved in the drafting of checklists and monitoring progress. Checklists should be complemented by descriptive comments.

Example: **PROBLEM SOLVING/INVESTIGATION CHECKLIST**

Approach:
• How did students start? _____

• Did students use a systematic approach (planning, implement-ation and assessment?) _____

• Are goals met? _____

• Are students able to justify results? _____

Attitude
• Are students self-motivated? _____

• Are students independent? _____

• Are students willing to take risks? _____

Specific skill development
• Are students able to interpret data? _____

• Are students able to represent information in an effective way? _____

• Are calculations correct? _____

The information gathered from this checklist should be used for further planning.

CO-OPERATIVE LEARNING SKILLS CHECKLIST

Task skills		Social skills		Work skills	
staying on task	☐	listening to others	☐	self-motivated	☐
finishing task		using quiet voice	☐	independent	☐
following directions	☐	taking turns	☐	enthusiastic participant	☐
recording ideas		using names	☐	willing to take risks	☐
staying in groups	☐	asking questions	☐	creative thinking	
sharing materials		sharing ideas	☐	logical thinking	
watching time	☐	justifying ideas	☐	displays confidence	☐
		reporting ideas	☐		
		asking for help	☐		
		helping others	☐		
		critical thinking	☐		
		achieving group consensus	☐		

(Wilson & Egeberg 1989)

THINGS TO DO

• Draw up a checklist of skills you want students to learn and trial this with a group of students during an appropriate activity.

• Ask students to use similar checklists for their self- or peer evaluation.

• Use your planned understandings as a checklist.

CUMULATIVE RECORD KEEPING

Keeping samples of work, checklists, anecdotal notes and self-assessment records together is an effective way of accumulating an on-going profile of each student's understandings, strengths and weaknesses.

We need to make time to reflect on the data collected in the profile for curriculum purposes and share such materials with students from time to time. During such discussions students may also wish to comment on their progress or signal the types of actions they intend to take. If students have access to their own files they can add work themselves and gauge their own development. They can, for example, make a comparison between initial generalisations and reworked generalisations:

I am happy about ____ now, but now I need to work on ____ .

Remember that only some records are of long term use, others are dispensable and should be discarded when they outlive their usefulness.

ASSESSING CONCEPTS AND THINKING PROCESSES

CONCEPT MAPPING

Concept maps, also known as mind maps and semantic webs, are a way to represent the links or relationships between concepts graphically. Concept mapping is a useful strategy for planning and assessment. When students draw a concept map they often show you what they know about the field of knowledge on which the unit is based.

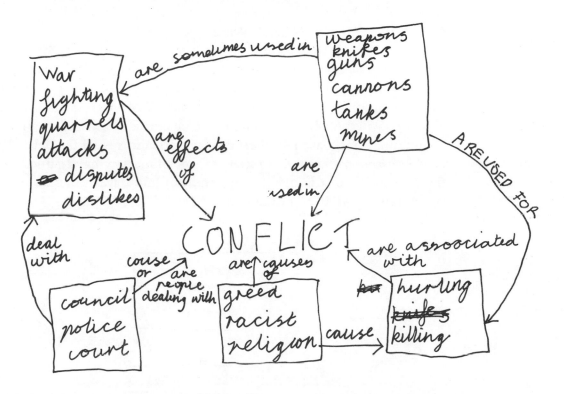

As concept maps are based on students' prior knowledge and an understanding of the work completed, their concept maps can be inaccurate. Even when students and teachers use the same language, we cannot assume that they necessarily have the same understanding of the words. Further, we should not conclude that the inability to explain a concept means that it is not understood:

> . . . *we cannot assume that because a person lacks the language to articulate the concept that the person does not have a grasp of the concept. (Adams 1991, p.2)*

As students work on their concept maps, and at various stages of refinement, teachers need to take time to discuss any misunderstandings.

Concept maps can be taught to students of all ages. Stice (1987) examined the potential of concept mapping with students in kindergarten through to Year 5. Concept mapping was found to increase students' ability to organise and represent their thoughts. Novak (1988) explains that students who learn meaningfully acquire, retain, and use knowledge to construct better organised maps than those who learn by rote.

HOW TO USE CONCEPT MAPS

Constructing a class/group concept map is a useful way of getting students to talk about their understanding of concepts. Students should be given the opportunity to share maps together, discussing with peers their inclusion, omission and placement of words. With practice, students will be able to construct concept maps using their own terminology and based on their own understandings of the field. This is where students are able to show the meaning they have gained from their experiences. The following concept map was constructed by students in Year 6 at Eltham East Primary School.

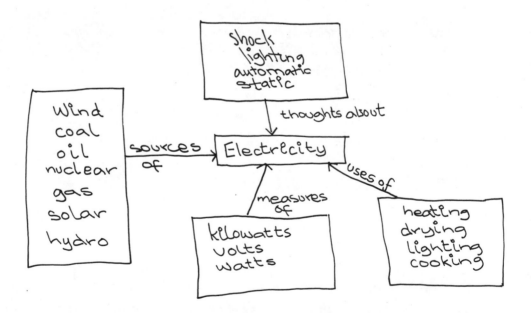

This concept map shows the students' understanding of electricity. They have been able to group together certain key words. At a later stage in the unit, students would be asked to make some connections between the groups.

During the tuning in stage, we can ask students to complete a mapping exercise to gain insights into what they already know about the topic. If students find the exercise difficult it may be because of lack of understanding or inadequate prior knowledge of the field, and this will indicate material that may need to be covered or revised before the shared experience. Experiences can be planned accordingly. Concept mapping exercises may be repeated during or after the unit of work to consolidate, revise and/or determine understanding of the work completed. Slow progress may indicate that teaching methods need to be questioned. As well as enhancing meaningful student learning, concept mapping can add to the teacher's repertoire of planning and assessment techniques.

THINGS TO DO

- Before, during or after a unit, ask students to brainstorm words about a topic or a major concept. Use arrows and linking words to show connections within it.
- Try mapping selected key words related to the topic, such as animals, mammals, cats, dogs, reptiles, snails, lizards, fur, etc. (This is useful with young or inexperienced mappers but it has less value in telling you what students already know.)

CLOZE

Cloze is not just the process of 'filling the gap'. By selecting and deleting certain words the teacher can assess knowledge of the topic and the linguistic cues used. This technique has many possibilities across the curriculum, in terms of finding information about students' understandings and ideas. Cloze can also be used before and after a unit of work to gauge a change in beliefs, attitudes or values.

THINGS TO DO
- Ask students to design cloze activities for other class members.

RANKING EXERCISES

Ranking exercises can be used to encourage reflection, discussion and assessment of feelings and values. Students think about the item and then locate it on a scale from strong agreement to strong disagreement.

THINGS TO DO
- Use your planned understandings to gauge students' feeling and values about an issue. You may need to change your wording slightly as in the first example below. In this case, the teacher's understanding was: *People can recycle and reuse much of their rubbish.*

  Students in Lesley Wing Jan's class at Eltham East Primary School were asked to rank the following statements about the natural environment:
- People should recycle their paper, metal, food scraps and glass.

- People can have positive and negative effects on the natural environment.
- Helping the environment often means personal sacrifices.

These were some of the students' responses:

<u>What's your opinion?</u> Eloise

- People should recycle their paper, metal, food scraps and glass

Strongly Agree   Agree   I   Disagree   Strongly Disagree

Some adults don't bother recycling
because they won't be around when the
world gets polluted and rubbish
everywhere

EVALUATING WHAT TEACHERS DO
CHOOSING RESOURCES

The resources we choose help to define for students the essential ideas about the world that we think are worth knowing. Linked with these ideas are values and attitudes about social class, gender, ethnicity and age. We have to assess the range of cultural diversity within our selected resources and attempt to redress any imbalances through inclusive strategies and the resistance of stereotypes. We need to choose resources which are rich in information about the particular topic and which cater for difference. We must also give students models of how to represent a range of ideas, or different perspectives on an issue.

USING RESOURCES

The way we use resources often determines their effectiveness in sustaining students' learning. Resources should allow students to make connections with their own prior knowledge and experiences, but they also need to take them beyond their current knowledge base. When using particular resources, we need to consider what questions we will ask; what grouping strategies we will adopt to allow students to interact; what records of students' learning will be kept; and how we will display or refer back to these resources throughout the unit.

The criteria used for the selection and evaluation of resources and for making program decisions often will be similar. The key question is: *Are they rich enough to develop understandings?* Other considerations include: *Do programs/resources cater for:*

- the range of students' abilities and learning styles

- students from different backgrounds

Are programs/resources:

- interesting
- challenging
- gender inclusive
- open-ended and flexible
- up-to-date

Do programs/resources encourage:

- active learning
- a range of outcomes
- student talk
- group work
- values clarification
- alternative viewpoints
- risk taking and exploration of ideas

Is there a balance between whole class, small group, individual, active and quiet activities?

EVALUATING THE SELECTION AND USE OF RESOURCES

Although there is no single resource most appropriate for any integrated curriculum unit, some units will require specific resources. Ideally, a variety of resources should be available for every unit of work to broaden and enrich students' experiences and to allow data to be processed/presented in a variety of ways. We need to ask which resources will contain sufficiently rich information to qualify as a shared experience and which resources will qualify as related experiences.

Some of these might include:

- **Environment**   The schoolground, local parks, library, street, shopping centre, other schools, museums, galleries, etc.
- **People**   Parents, local community members, elderly people, students.
- **Audiovisual materials**   Videos, music, photographs, maps, slides, etc.
- **Artefacts**   Paintings, clothing, tools.
- **Printed materials**   Texts, books, newspapers.
- **Computer software**

LISTEN AND WE SHALL LEARN: QUESTIONING WITH A DUAL PURPOSE

If learning is to be meaningful it needs to be linked to the learners' existing knowledge. The implication for teachers' questioning is that it should tap what is already known, and also develop new ideas. The answers given by students can provide us with useful information about what students know. The quality of responses will be influenced by our questioning techniques.

Unfortunately, we often restrict students' answers by asking closed questions where only one answer is acceptable, for example *How many states are there in Australia?* We often give limited time for responses and ask lower level questions based on simple recall. Within an integrated curriculum there are many opportunities to develop higher level thinking skills. We should plan for this, and monitor the types of questions we ask. Well thought out questions should help learning and provide teachers with assessment information:

> *The ability of the teacher to ask questions that challenge and extend students' thinking is vitally important to an inquiry approach to learning. (Ministry of Education, Victoria 1988a, p.49).*

Bloom's taxonomy gives us a framework for developing thinking skills that can sometimes be neglected in the curriculum:

BLOOM'S TAXONOMY	MEANING	PREREQUISITES	SAMPLE QUESTIONS AND THINKING STARTERS	PERFORMANCE INDICATORS
Knowledge	recall	memory	• Who said/did? • Describe what happened . . .	• restate • name • list
Comprehension	understanding of	rewording	• Write in your own words • Distinguish between . . .	• describe in own words • summarise • argue
Application	applying knowledge or rule to another situation	classifying, choice making	• Think of another time when . . . • Can you relate to . . .?	• solve • plan • using idea again
Analysis	pull information apart, explore ideas/relationships	identify causes/ draw conclusions	What are other outcomes/problems of . . .?	• clarifying • dividing inform-ation into bits • design • reconstruct
Synthesis	put parts together/ create new idea	prediction, problem solving	• Devise your own • Think of some solutions	• design • reconstruct
Evaluation	judge decisions	opinions	• Make a judgement • How would you have done it?	• supporting decision • justifying choice

(Adapted from Ministry of Education, Victoria, 1986).

These thinking processes were applied to *The Rainbow Serpent,* a text used as part of the integrated topic, 'Changing Australia as seen through literature', in a Year 6 classroom.

Comprehension
Why do you think the Rainbow Serpent followed the path that he did?

Application
If the Rainbow Serpent came to Eltham now what might he teach you?

Analysis
Why did the Rainbow Serpent seek his tribe?

Synthesis
What would happen if the Rainbow Serpent was a different type of animal? (Choose an animal and tell your tale.)

Evaluation
Do you think it was okay for the Rainbow Serpent to destroy the mountain when he had his stomach split open? Why?

Students found these questions challenging because, in their words, 'They are all like quiz questions, not straight from the book, they need an opinion.' They also required students to draw upon their knowledge of the world. During discussions with the group responding to the synthesis question, the students spoke of the features of animals and the feasibility of substituting for the serpent. This is their response:

WHAT WOULD HAVE HAPPENED IF THE SERPENT HAD BEEN A DIFFERENT TYPE OF ANIMAL?

No other animal could replace the Rainbow Serpent because if it was a 4 legged animal it could not create mountains, valleys, lagoons and rivers

Carly, Clare O, Leeba, Rajiv, Thihan

TIIINGS TO DO

- Pose questions based on the different thinking processes.
- Ask students to write their own questions, activities, tests and cloze activities.
- Increase 'wait time' after asking questions and after responses. Observe the changes in:
  - length of answers
  - number of volunteers offering to answer
  - number of questions that students initiate
  - responses using higher levels of thinking skills
- Ask students to ask questions of you and each other. You'll be amazed! Here are some examples from Year 6 at Eltham East Primary School:
  - How did this session help us with our learning?
  - Why do people do such cruel things to other living things?
  - Why do women prefer to be teachers than men?
  - Why is the universe so diverse and complex although it was made by a natural reaction?

GATHERING FEEDBACK FROM AND REPORTING TO OTHERS

A scene from an excursion to the Victoria Market.

As well as teacher self-assessment, there are strategies teachers can use to elicit comment from other teachers, parents and students. It will not always be possible to involve parents and other teachers in the program as much as you would like to, but there are ways to 'keep them in touch'. Some teachers like to send home class newspapers with information about current classroom happenings and suggestions of ways that parents can help.

A scene from an excursion to Sovereign Hill.

CLASSROOM NEWSLETTER

We are studying changes in school life over the last 100 years. Does anyone have any old books or photos they could lend us? We would also welcome a parent, grandparent or friend to speak to us about their experiences.

Yesterday we played old games, I think the computer is a much better toy. Mrs Smith said that they didn't have a computer in the old days when she was a kid. **Troy**

PHOTOGRAPHIC OR VISUAL RECORDS

By taking photographs or video recordings during a unit of work, experiences can be represented in a concrete way and visual way. The photographs can be collected in a class book to be shared with others. In a similar way, you or the students can set up class displays of students' work. These concrete examples of classroom activities can be used to complement other forms of assessment data such as checklists, anecdotal notes and files when reporting to parents, students and administrators.

TEACHER SELF-ASSESSMENT

We need to reflect upon our own practices to ensure that the program, strategies and resources are appropriate. Like student assessment, effective teacher assessment is a continuous process and forms the basis for further planning. Assessment results are only effective if you use them to make informed choices when planning what and how to teach.

> . . . *frequently we assess to no purpose; collecting information we already possess, do not need, or information upon which we will never act. (Clark 1988, p.1)*

Teacher reflection should include personal assessment, for example:
* Did the strategies help to clarify/extend understandings?
* How did I help the students to learn?
* Can I identify every student's strengths and weaknesses?
* Was my feedback appropriate?
* How do I provide a supportive learning environment?
* Do I enable students to be part of the decision making process?
* Do I make time for the things that I value?

Keeping a journal is one way to ponder these questions, and others. It is a way of documenting what you do, to clarify your beliefs and to examine how your efforts meet your aims.

Working with colleagues in team teaching situations or as part of a support group encourages continual and immediate reflection and refinement. Planning, teaching and sharing resources with others can be a very effective use of time. Just as we hope to promote meta-cognitive skills in students, we should aim to explicitly reflect upon and analyse our own teaching practice.

Monitoring what you do, and knowing how and why you do it, is important for improving practice.

A BALANCED PROGRAM: WHAT ABOUT SKILLS?

In an integrated curriculum, all activities are chosen to develop understandings of the topic. But as integrated curriculum is not a total curriculum, there are times when it is necessary to move out of the unit in order to teach skills. For example, in order to process mathematical data using large numbers, students must have an understanding of how to use a calculator and to estimate 'likely' results. Sometimes it is possible to do this within the context of the unit. At other times, skills need to developed systematically within the relevant curriculum program.

There are also times when teaching opportunities arising from student interests and needs will shift the focus from the integrated topic. Teachers are in the best position to decide which avenues will enrich or distract learners. We can never accurately predict students' interests and questions, and we must cater for this in our planning. Ongoing assessment strategies, such as those outlined above, will show when we need to modify our plans, understandings, and information about student learning, teaching strategies, resources and the classroom environment. Necessary interventions or changes of direction or emphasis can be carried out as the need arises.

PUTTING TESTING IN ITS PLACE

In the past, prepared tests have been used to assess students' knowledge of isolated facts and skills. The use of these tests has influenced our teaching practices and our reporting procedures.

There are several reasons why tests have been considered attractive:
- tests give us a numerical figure with which we can make comparisons
- tests give quick results
- tests are meant to be objective
- testing has been used for years to gauge students' progress

Unfortunately, these reasons are neither educationally sound nor accurate.

The scope of what students learn cannot be determined by marks on a test paper. Standardised tests cannot recognise the development of thought processes, co-operative problem-solving or decision-making skills. We must gauge what students know and learn using a variety of strategies which begin during tuning in activities. We must make assessment an integral part of units of work.

What elements of an integrated curriculum can we test? How can we test complex processes like thinking? How would you rate an idea? Assessment techniques must be appropriate to skills and understandings taught; the link between planning, activities and assessment is vital.

With changes in content and strategies, many existing assessment techniques are not appropriate or broad enough to provide information to teachers, students, parents and administrators. Assessment techniques need to reflect the new emphasis on learning that is meaningful and that can be applied in real life. To provide for the needs and interests of every student, we require useful and usable assessment techniques and we must make time for reflection and action.

THINGS TO DO
- Make a checklist of the skills/concepts you wish to develop in your integrated unit. Keep a running tally by highlighting those you cover at the end of each week. (Note those neglected for next week or next unit.)
- Give your students a list of the skills and ask them to keep their own records.
- Use questions designed for tests as a part of other activities, for example, discussions, co-operative group activities, quizzes and games.
- Ask students to design tests/cloze activities for each other. (Initially, students will ask basic recall questions, but with direction and modelling they can form questions that require higher order thinking skills.)

Here is a test designed by a group of Year 6 students as part of the unit 'Changing Melbourne':

1 Give two reasons why the Yarra River shrank.

2 Do you think the Yarra River will ever increase in size?

3 Why did the white people clear the land?

4 In December 1855 a child was born, his name was John, what was his surname?

5 Who was the first child born to: a blacksmith, a bushranger or a farmer?

6 Why did the bushrangers choose St Kilda Road as their target?

CONCLUSION

The responsibility of a teacher is indeed daunting. What we do has a significant impact on the lives of others. When we teach we must conscientiously seek to understand how we influence students' lives, and one important way is through the variety of assessment procedures we use. We are in the business of making choices; we do so every day on behalf of our learners when we consider appropriate topics, content, understandings, skills, teaching strategies, resources and assessment techniques.

To cope with the challenge of active education we must become keen kidwatchers and pattern detectors if we are to positively contribute to students' learning. An integrated approach to teaching and learning offers us many opportunities to be active inquirers and learners along with our students.

6
BRINGING ABOUT CURRICULUM CHANGE

Neville Johnson draws together his experiences of working with teachers, principals and consultants in bringing about curriculum change in schools and classrooms. He aims to achieve teacher, classroom and school improvement which may lead to more effective teaching and learning outcomes. In doing so, he synthesises much of the research literature on teachers and change and considers the implications of this growing body of knowledge for school action plans.

◆

There are many legitimate routes to teacher, classroom and school improvement, and an integrated approach to curriculum design and implementation is one. The ultimate purpose of any classroom or school improvement is to increase the quality of teaching and learning. An integrated approach to curriculum is an excellent vehicle, catalyst and point of departure for teachers wishing to think about the theory and practice of learning and teaching and for schools considering a focus for a whole school development plan.

A number of people have a stake in the way a school or classroom operates, and any proposal for change will affect them all. These stakeholders include students, parents, teachers and administrators and each brings to the situation particular views of the purposes of schooling and what teaching involves. These views, in turn, influence responses to the proposal for change.

A proposal to improve teaching and learning affects organisations as well as individuals. The organisation affected may be the whole school or, in the case of a larger institution, sections within the school. A school has been likened to a spider web in that many different kinds of people are tied together by organisational and personal threads in a form of a 'web'. If a few threads of a spider's web are touched the whole web shakes. Similarly, when a proposal for change influences individuals there are ramifications for sections within the school as well as for the whole school. It is crucial to realise that individuals influence organisations and organisations influence the extent and nature of individual change.

There are two obvious responses available to individuals and organisations when they are asked to consider movement towards an integrated approach to curriculum design and implementation. They may actively or passively reject the proposal, or the proposal may be accepted. If accepted, curriculum change is not an event but a **process** which occurs over time and which most researchers currently believe proceeds through three broad stages:

- **Stage 1,** named variously **adoption,** initiation or mobilisation is the initial sign of acceptance of a proposal for change which culminates in the decision to use or undertake the change.
- **Stage 2,** called **initial implementation,** includes the beginning attempts to put the proposal into practice.
- **Stage 3,** labelled **continuation of implementation**, maintenance, incorporation, or institutionalisation is concerned with sustaining the implementation of the change.

This chapter considers these stages of the change process in relation to both **individual teachers** wishing to introduce a more integrated approach to curriculum and **schools** considering integrated curriculum as part of their whole school improvement plan.

BRINGING ABOUT CHANGE IN THE CLASSROOM: INDIVIDUAL TEACHER CHANGE

Louise is in her eighth year of teaching. She has recently upgraded her qualifications to complete her B.Ed (Primary) fourth year on a part-time basis. In this course she participated in the subject 'Curriculum Integration' and developed an integrated curriculum unit suited to the needs of her students. She is about to implement this unit and, in doing so, use a more integrated approach to her teaching and learning strategies. Louise is faced with the challenge of getting started, and is developing her own plan of action in her classroom.

There are no recipes for implementing change and improvement in the classroom, but there are some guidelines, based on research studies and the collective wisdom gathered by observing a great number of successful classroom practitioners who have travelled similar pathways and shared their successes, anxieties and constraints. These guidelines are:

1 Start from where you are at.
2 Begin with a small change in classroom practice.
3 Work simultaneously on content, learning processes, classroom learning experiences and teaching/learning tactics and strategies.
4 Practise reflection in action, on action and about action.

5 Find a friend to work with.
6 Seek school support.

1 START FROM WHERE YOU ARE AT

Most action planning strategies suggest that before deciding on action, it is important to take stock of the existing situation. This guideline urges the teacher contemplating an integrated approach to curriculum in their classroom to spend time evaluating where they are at before making any moves.

Current values, expectations and practice are the base upon which teachers should build. Teachers often find it difficult to articulate what they stand for, and how and why they work in classrooms the way they do. Teaching is such a demanding and complex occupation that time for reflection on values, purpose and practice is difficult to find or make. Much of a teacher's action is habit and custom that has been given the test of 'defensibility'. That is, teachers should periodically ask of their practice: 'Can I defend this practice in the light of what is now known about effective learning and quality teaching?'

Teachers who are reading this book will be able to test their current values, expectations and practice against the assertions of what comprises effective learning and quality teaching in an integrated curriculum approach. Juxtaposing your current situation with the preferred position advocated in this book should allow you to identify the strengths of your present practice and aspects that, if worked on, could lead to improved practice. When undertaking this process there are three possible scenarios:

- An evaluation of the present situation could lead some teachers to the conclusion that they currently use a curriculum design approach that could best be termed **separated.** That is, they currently plan and implement the curriculum in clearly distinguished blocks of activities such as handwriting, mathematics, spelling, art, science, creative writing, social sciences . . . each activity essentially standing alone although connections between activities are sometimes made explicit.

- Others may conclude that they presently use a curriculum design approach that could be described as **related**. These teachers may use a theme to which many activities relate while still retaining an entity of their own. Thus, if the theme is 'The Sea', poems on this theme are read, word study explores words arising from the theme and stories are written, social studies information and concepts related to the theme are investigated, and so on

- Some teachers may conclude, after taking stock of their current approach, that they already embrace many of the values and practices referred to as **integrated** in this book. These teachers perhaps take a topic as a focus and make explicit the relevant understandings to be explored and demonstrated by the students. In classroom practice, activities flow into one another with information gathered in one activity being processed in others. Similarly, language, art and mathematics are used to gather information, to make sense of what has been learned and to tell others about it.

For each teacher this process of evaluation will reveal different starting points. For some, substantial new learning will have to take place while for others fine-tuning of existing approaches will be sufficient. With the essence of what constitutes integrated curriculum design and implementation in mind, each teacher's challenge is to form, over time, their own concept of 'integrated learning' — one that suits their particular situation.

As well as taking stock of one's personal values, expectations and practice, this guideline urges teachers to consider the present situation in their school before deciding on action. There is substantial support for the claim that teacher change will be severely constrained if the school organisational climate and arrangements do not support the adjustments in role, function, culture and structure that are needed for lasting change. If the school environment is low in the element of trust then the teacher is well advised to make cautious plans. In contrast, if the school environment is judged to be supportive and high in trust then the teacher's plans can be more open. It is essential that the teacher is sensitive to the guiding beliefs and expectations evident in the way the school operates and strives to relate appropriately to other people by not overstepping accepted boundaries.

2 BEGIN WITH SMALL CHANGES

When beginning to implement change, the advice is often given to 'think big, but start small'. For many teachers, changing to an integrated curriculum approach is 'big' in the sense that quite a significant movement in attitudes and practice of stakeholders (students, adult advocates of students, teacher and colleagues) is required for successful implementation. This guideline cautions against being too ambitious. Be prepared to take risks and try out new practice, but do it on a small scale.

Our framework of attitudes and beliefs is our main source of security. Other people trying to change us are bound to make us feel insecure, but if we experience something new for ourselves then we might be prepared to modify our attitudes in the light of this experience. Teachers may not really know how they feel about an integrated approach to curriculum until they have used it and considered its impact. Guskey (1985) asserts that if teachers are prepared to make small changes in their classroom practice, and if that change has a positive impact on learning and teaching, then they will be likely to take the next step. Also, the cumulative experience of successful small changes is very likely to lead in the long term to quite significant change in attitudes.

Teachers collaboratively planning changes to their practice.

We know that change in practice is accompanied by stress and anxiety, especially in the early stages of the process. Every time teachers try something different they are taking a risk. It is important to remember that a new practice in the classroom is likely to be new for both students and the teacher. This is another reason for 'starting small', trying it out on a small scale, so that all the people involved are given time to build the confidence, skills and knowledge required to work in the new way.

3 WORK SIMULTANEOUSLY

When implementing an integrated curriculum approach it is important that teachers and students work on four components together: content, learning processes, learning experiences and teaching/learning strategies.

If students experience quality learning experiences in their classrooms and elsewhere, they are more likely to achieve a wide range of content, process and attitudinal outcomes. If these learning experiences are made explicit to them, they build their confidence, knowledge and skills and develop expanded learning styles. The stronger the students are, and the more tools they possess, the more effective has been the teaching.

Effective student learning is obviously closely linked to the quality of teaching provided. Students are more likely to make more sense of their world and refine learning strategies if their teachers use a variety of approaches to teaching that require engagement in content and practice of processes.

However, teachers will only teach in such a variety of ways if they possess a repertoire of teaching strategies. Such teachers believe that there are many powerful approaches to teaching designed to bring about particular kinds of learning and to help students become more effective learners. They believe that combinations of teaching approaches can have a more dramatic effect than any one could have alone. They believe that they need to be able to identify these approaches and select the ones that are appropriate to support the achievement of learning outcomes being valued, the curriculum materials/environments available and student preferences and skills.

Teachers implementing integrated curriculum designs use a variety of simple and complex co-operative learning strategies, and offer students the option of working independently. They provide students with a choice of media and symbol systems with which to gather, process and present information. They use concept learning techniques such as concept attainment, concept formation and generalisation and concept mapping to help students attain and invent concepts and make statements of understanding.

These teachers commit to continuous learning and improvement and to the mastery of a repertoire of approaches to teaching and learning. When teaching and learning strategies, worthwhile learning experiences, attention to content and learning processes all function in partnership, the chances of achieving an effective classroom learning environment are dramatically increased.

4 PRACTISE REFLECTION

This guideline urges teachers engaged in the process of change in their classrooms to commit to systematic and continuous reflection in, on and about their practice. In the early stages of the change process, it is natural that much of a teacher's thinking will be about the practicalities of classroom action. Donald Schon (1987) suggests the concept of the 'reflective practitioner' as a way of encouraging people in professions such as teaching to reflect critically on the purpose and value of their practice as well as the logistics. Teachers usually find this more possible during the continuation stage of the change process.

There are many techniques for developing reflective practice, including writing in diaries and journals, professional reading, involvement in teacher interest and support groups, undertaking classroom research and writing retrospectives on classroom projects.

5 FIND A FRIEND TO WORK WITH

As the teacher begins to try out integrated curriculum approaches it is important to find a colleague to work with. With the aid of a few trusted friends, a good idea or two and the use of initiative, success is almost assured. Fullan and Hargreaves (1991) argue that working with others is essential to individual development but caution against superficial and wasteful forms of collaboration, and of collaboration in the service of ends you regard as questionable, impractical or indefensible.

There are many possible steps to take: talk to a colleague about the success or otherwise of the first step taken towards curriculum integration; plan an integrated unit together; work as a teaching partner with the teacher-librarian and/or other specialists; offer to have a student teacher in your room; invite a trusted colleague to watch you teach or be your mentor.

Teachers jointly planning understandings for their unit.

6 SEEK SCHOOL SUPPORT

It is axiomatic that there can be no curriculum change without individual teacher and classroom change. However, the evidence suggests that without the encouragement and support of the school, individual teachers find it difficult to sustain the energy required to weather the ups and downs associated with the implementation of a new classroom approach. If the formal leadership of the school is supportive of teacher growth, and encourages classroom and school improvement, then it is more likely that a teacher's move towards an integrated approach to curriculum will be acknowledged and may even be considered as a focus for school-wide implementation.

These guidelines are best seen as the foundation of the teacher's action plan for implementation of an integrated curriculum approach. They will be most effective if practised in combination, because they complement and build on each other. It is impossible to address separately the many different situations that teachers could face. Plans for action cannot be standardised. It is through informed experimentation, pursuing promising directions, and refining initial arrangements and practices that the most headway will be made. Therefore, **action** in trying out new approaches is imperative to successful initial implementation.

BRINGING ABOUT CHANGE IN THE SCHOOL: WHOLE SCHOOL IMPROVEMENT AND CHANGE

Christine is the principal of a metropolitan primary school with an enrolment of 250 students and twelve teachers. She has been at the school for 18 months during which time she has managed, with the support of several active members of staff, to reach the stage where there is general acceptance of the need to explore some new ways of teaching and learning. There is agreement on the value of building a whole school plan that will include a focus for school and classroom improvement and change. The staff is faced with the daunting task of selecting a curriculum focus and bringing about the change.

Effective schools have always made plans. These include plans to promote student learning (curriculum development), plans to establish the desired school norms, procedures and roles (organisational development) and plans to ensure staff support and learning (professional development). In recent years, the emphasis has been on the need for these plans to be made collaboratively by involving, in appropriate ways, all the stakeholders of schooling. The need to document the plans has been stressed in an effort to enable greater fidelity during the implementation of the plans and to help review outcomes and processes.

This emphasis on the development and documentation of what is named variously Total School Plan, School Review and Development Plan, or Whole School Plan has led school communities to consider their priorities carefully. It is sensible that in such a plan the majority of resources and energy are directed to the maintenance of ongoing projects, but schools are being encouraged to invest some of their resources and energy in school improvement and change. It is argued that without such a commitment the school is in danger of maintaining the status quo and locking into the habit and custom without first examining the social, political and educational changes that are taking place around them.

The selection of the focus for curriculum improvement and change is possibly the single most important decision that the school staff makes. The following aspects need to be considered:

• It should follow an intensive review of the present curriculum which includes identification of the current strengths of the school program, and aspects that need to be worked on.

- It preferably builds on an existing 'head of steam' in the curriculum area.
- It must be defensible in terms of being 'worth doing' given current knowledge of learning and teaching, and school and system priorities.
- It should pass the test of 'strategic gain', that is, work on the selected change should have the greatest pay-off for student learning for the least amount of effort.

A decision to implement an integrated curriculum approach would meet these criteria and be an appropriate focus for school improvement. A careful plan that has whole school, classroom and teacher professional development components is required. Figure 6.1 shows the relationship between the important elements of such a plan.

Central to bringing about change in the school and classrooms is a well-planned and implemented teacher professional development program. Teacher learning is the key to successful adoption and implementation of the change. It is the teachers who will need to work on their repertoire of teaching strategies and tactics in a reflective, collaborative and systematic way if classroom and school improvement is to take place. It is teacher attitudes and beliefs about teaching and learning that will be challenged by successful implementation of an integrated approach to curriculum.

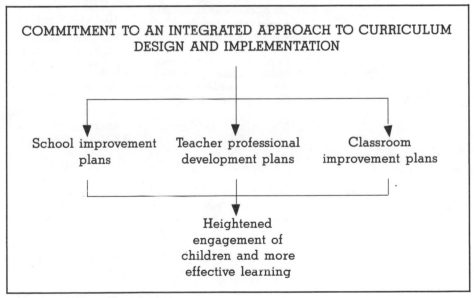

Figure 6.1: Elements of a plan to implement an integrated approach to curriculum

The relationship between the stages of the change process, teacher professional development action and important guiding principles is summarised in figure 6.2, and is explained in more detail in what follows.

STAGE	GUIDELINES	PROFESSIONAL DEVELOPMENT ACTION
1 Adoption **The initial sign of acceptance of a change proposal which culminates in the decision to undertake the change.** At this stage, plans are made to raise staff awareness of the power, purpose and nature of an integrated curriculum approach.	Begin by having teachers acknowledging and valuing their own current practice and identifying the characteristics of the proposed curriculum change. Carefully design a teacher professional development program. Preferably adopt the change as a whole school focus	Sensitising activities Such activities are designed to alert staff to the change. **Raising awareness event** A special whole staff occasion such as a curriculum pupil-free day devoted to the change proposal. **Follow-up work** Action plans are implemented to further explore the nature of the change and what it looks like in classroom practice.
2 Initial implementation Includes the beginning attempts to put into practice the change proposal. At this stage, teachers who are willing, try small changes towards an integrated curriculum approach in their classrooms.	**When new learning is required of teachers, appropriate learning conditions must be established and resources made available.** **Emphasise small changes in classroom practice and be prepared to work over a long time period.** **Co-operative/collaborative professional development strategies should be used.** **Professional development strategies should satisfy each teacher's needs for affiliation, achievement and influence.**	**Plan integrated units** Pairs or small groups of teachers work together to plan units of work. **Opportunities for talking and sharing practical ideas** Planned sharing opportunities such as 'tactic workshops' and 'this works for me', show and tell. **Watching each other teach** Carefully negotiated and voluntary observation in classrooms. **Problem-solving together** Action research approaches to systematically work on shared problems of implementation.
3 Continuation of implementation **Is concerned with sustaining the implementation of the change.** At this stage, care must be taken to consider evaluations of the initial implementation stage in order to reaffirm learnings, finetune practice and make necessary changes in direction.	Consider and take action on information from evaluation of initial implementation. **Acknowledge that curriculum change is often associated with change in attitudes towards teaching and learning.** **Remember, that teachers will be at different stages of concern and use of the change.**	**Planned review of initial implementation** Systematic reflection of implementation work **Action plans for continuation are constructed.** Teachers already involved must have the opportunity to plan further action. **Support teachers ready for initial implementation**

Figure 6.2: Relationship between stages of change, guidelines and professional action.

STAGE 1: ADOPTION

Raising awareness of the nature, purpose and potential of an integrated approach to curriculum

It is at this stage that the concept of an integrated curriculum is introduced for consideration and its characteristics explored in terms of implications for valued learning outcomes, teacher and student roles and relationships, and school and classroom resources, structures and processes. Teachers should be encouraged to consider their current classroom practice and beliefs about teaching and learning in relation to the concept of an integrated curriculum.

For some teachers there will be a 'match' between the information contained in the change proposal and their current understanding and practice of teaching and learning. These teachers are merely required to fine-tune or adapt existing beliefs, methods and skills to accommodate the proposal. Such learning is relatively easy to undertake.

However, for other teachers the move requires substantial new learning and additions to their existing teaching repertoire. There is a 'mismatch' between the information contained in the change proposal and their current understanding and practice. These teachers are often challenged by new information which requires them to value different learning outcomes, play new teaching roles, and display new teaching strategies and skills. Such change is likely to be threatening and difficult to implement.

These teachers fit the image of what Doyle and Ponder (1977) name the 'pragmatic sceptic'. The pragmatic sceptic's response to a change proposal is guided by the 'practicality ethic'. Three central components of the practicality ethic, and criteria that teachers appear to use to decide whether or not an innovation is 'practical' and, therefore, a candidate for adoption and implementation are:

- **instrumentality** — procedural clarity, depicting classroom contingencies
- **congruence** — degree of match between change proposal and teacher's existing classroom situation and personal preference in role/values
- **cost** — effort/return ratio that results when teacher weighs the ease with which the change can be implemented against the potential return it will yield.

Pragmatic sceptics are generally solid workers but are unlikely to seek out change. They usually support activities in areas that they are already comfortable in, but will oppose or withdraw from activities that threaten the status quo. They may appear to be quite supportive of new curriculum ideas while there is no pressure to change, but they revert to a sceptical orientation in the face of any change proposal. It is important to note that for this type of teacher, changes in attitudes or beliefs about new approaches to teaching usually follow rather than precede changes in teaching practice. New practices which lead to improved learning outcomes have a particularly profound effect on changing their attitudes.

· The guidelines for this stage of the change process include the following:

1 Begin by having teachers acknowledging and valuing their own current practice and identifying the characteristics of the proposed curriculum change

Current practice is the base on which teachers should build their professional development. If the professional development issue originates from outside the teacher's workplace then the teacher must be able to connect their practice with it to achieve success. This means that teachers must become aware of their existing teaching/learning repertoire and reflect upon it.

If teachers are to seriously consider changing the way they teach, they must be aware of the implications of specific changes for classroom practice. It is important that teachers identify the characteristics of the selected change proposal, noting the implications of each characteristic for school organisation and classroom practice. To do this, questions such as the following need to be asked:

- *What school structures and processes are required?*
  Are particular decision-making and communication structures/processes assumed?
- *What resources are needed for implementation?*
  Are particular human and material resources required?
  What learning outcomes are being valued?
  Are there particular social, information or thinking skills and processes included?
  Does the content include new information, concepts, principles or theories?
- *What is the role of the teacher?*
  How is the work of the teacher and his/her relationship with students and colleagues affected?
  What does the teacher have to do in the classroom?
  What teacher knowledge and skill is assumed?
- *What is the role of the student?*
  How is the work of the student and his/her relationship with the teacher and fellow students affected?
  What does the student have to do in the classroom?
  What student knowledge and skill is assumed?
- *What is the role of the principal and other school leaders?*
  How is the work of the principal and his/her relationship with students and colleagues affected?

What does the principal have to do in the school?

What principal knowledge and skill is assumed?

- *What is the role of parents?*

  How can parents support the implementation of the change?

  What parent attitude, knowledge and skill is assumed?

2 Carefully design a teacher professional development program

A series of development sessions, separated by intervals to allow teachers to try things (with access to collegial help and other resources), is far more powerful than even the most stimulating one-shot workshop or curriculum day. It follows that:

- professional development sessions need to be carefully introduced and sustained over a long period of time
- professional development sessions need to be woven into the very fabric of the school
- careful action plans need to be made by individual teachers and teams of teachers
- most of the professional development resourced by the school should support the implementation of the school improvement/development plan
- professional development (arrangements made to promote the professional growth of staff) is inextricably linked with arrangements made to promote student learning (curriculum development) and arrangements made to build the health of the school (organisation development).

Teachers at work as learners.

3 Preferably adopt the change as a whole school focus

Teachers must recognise the change as one worthy of attention. Adopting an integrated approach to the curriculum as the focus for improvement in the whole school plan recognises the worthiness of the change and this helps to ensure its success.

4 Work on 'information', 'approach' and 'setting' together

Fullan and Stiegelbauer (1991) identify three major sets of factors that must occur in mutually reinforcing ways for a change to be successfully implemented.

The **setting** for professional development should be characterised by:

- administrative support (particularly active support by the principal)
- ready access to, and the development of, internal and external personnel and material support services and networks
- deliberate opportunities and incentives for recurrent or career-long participation in professional learning
- a problem-solving orientation (not a blaming orientation).

The **approach** should be:

- collegial
- continuous
- person-centred
- interactive

The **information** provided should be seen as:

- practical, applicable, relevant and clear, given the particular 'reality' of the individuals involved.

A carefully designed professional development program based on these guidelines is needed if the pragmatic sceptics are to be persuaded to adopt or even begin implementation of the change. Such a plan should include the following actions:

SENSITISING ACTIVITIES

These are activities designed to alert staff to the change and could consist of videos of an integrated curriculum in action, brief talks by practitioners using the approach, and visits to classrooms where the approach is being used.

RAISING AWARENESS EVENT

This should be a special whole staff occasion such as a curriculum/pupil-free day devoted to the change proposal. Such an occasion must be planned with effective professional development principles in mind.

FOLLOW-UP WORK

One product from the inservice day should be a set of action plans aimed at three levels: individual teacher, teams of teachers, and whole school. These plans should focus on the next steps to be taken to explore the nature of the change and what effective classroom practice looks like. The decision of whether or not to adopt the change should be formally taken once a clear picture of the change has been achieved.

STAGE 2: INITIAL IMPLEMENTATION

The beginning attempts to put into practice an integrated curriculum approach

At this stage, teachers who are willing attempt small changes towards an integrated curriculum approach in their classroom. Guidelines for this stage of the change process are as follows:

1 When new learning is required of teachers, appropriate learning conditions must be established and resources made available

Effective teacher learning requires opportunities for theory, modelling and demonstration, practice, feedback, and application in the workplace, along with ongoing colleague 'coaching' support and time for systematic reflection.

Brian Cambourne's (1988) conditions of literacy learning are as relevant to teacher learning (engagement in professional development) as to student/young adult learning. Consider what this list would look like if rewritten for teachers learning about an integrated approach to curriculum:

- Teachers need to be immersed in an environment that values and practises an integrated approach to curriculum.
- Teachers benefit from demonstrations, explanations and models which enable them to see how the classroom practice works.
- Teachers are influenced by the expectations of those around them, especially those they respect.
- Teachers grow in self-reliance if allowed to be involved in the decision making and share responsibility for the 'when and how' of the implementation of an integrated approach.
- Teachers must have time and opportunities in realistic situations to practise or use their developing control over what they are learning.
- Teachers work confidently when assured that their learning is not 'copied correctness' (fidelity to someone else's view of the correct way to work). Rather, approximation/mutual adaption to the change proposal should be encouraged through the process of trial and error improvement.
- Teachers are upheld in their implementation efforts (acknowledged and supported), when those around them respond with interest to their ideas and practice.

2 Emphasise small changes in classroom practice and be prepared to work over a long time period

In the first section of this chapter, teachers undertaking initial implementation of a new way of working were cautioned to begin with small changes. If teachers can be persuaded to make small changes in classroom practice, and these changes have positive outcomes for student learning and/or teacher teaching, then teachers are quite likely to try another small classroom change. Over a long period of time, quite substantial changes in teaching and learning may result.

3 Co-operative/collaborative professional development strategies should be used

Co-operative professional development is an approach to teacher learning in which the teacher plays an active role in deciding the needs to which inservice activities must respond and the knowledge and skills which must be learned. It is based on concrete experiences of teachers in schools and classrooms and often involves collaborative analysis of teacher roles and actions. It can take many forms but the main options and distinguishing features include the following:

- The teacher actively participates in the professional development process, constructing his or her own knowledge and being an agent of change.
- The expertise of the teacher is acknowledged and used in directing the professional development agenda.
- Teachers are encouraged to reflect on the concrete experiences of working with students in classrooms and schools.
- Although based on individual teacher reflection in action, co-operative professional development is often structured by a group of teachers working collectively to solve problems and to learn from each other.
- Outsiders work as facilitators and resource persons, offering their expertise as appropriate to the situation or as requested by the teachers.
- Joint teacher decisions extend beyond sharing of resources, teaching ideas and other practicalities to include critical reflection of the purpose and value of what is taught, and how it is taught in classrooms.
- Teachers are fundamentally accountable because they talk together about action and evaluate their work.

4 Professional development strategies should satisfy each teacher's needs for affiliation, achievement and influence

A review of the literature suggests that people expend their energy, care about and invest their emotion in search of three things: achievement, affiliation and influence.

ACHIEVEMENT
Individuals act to maximise their chances of being successful. They choose between behaviours that produce greater or lesser achievements.

The motivation to achieve leads people to take on challenges and to strive to do their best.

AFFILIATION
Individuals act to maximise their chances experiencing friendship. They choose behaviours that are helpful and express love, or those that are obstructive and express hate. The motivation to affiliate leads people to join together in warm and caring relationships.

INFLUENCE
Individuals act to maximise their chances of exerting influence over their own fates. They choose behaviours that evidence mastery over the world around them, or acquiescence (knuckling under) to the will of others. The motivation to influence leads people to demand the right to decide some things for themselves and to have their view acknowledged.

Another way of understanding these three primary human motives is to think about the 'feeling' words that get attached to them when the are met and when they are frustrated:

- When achievement motives are met . . . people feel competent, adequate, successful.
- When affiliative motives are met . . . people feel loved, cared about, part of the group.
- When influence motives are met . . . people feel powerful and 'on top of things'.

- When achievement motives are frustrated . . . people feel incompetent, bumbling, unsuccessful.
- When affiliative motives are frustrated . . . people feel lonely, ostracised, forced into solitude.
- When influence motives are frustrated . . . people feel powerless, 'snowed under', dominated.

Each teacher brings to the process of professional development pre-existing knowledge, attitudes, and ideas of professional role and the teaching world. This framework or 'cage' should be acknowledged, valued and used if professional development activities are to be successful in terms of improved teacher learning (and consequently student learning) and greater empowerment of teachers. If teachers are to be committed to professional development then their need for achievement, affiliation, and influence must be satisfied in the professional development process:

Professional development actions at this stage include:

PLANNING INTEGRATED UNITS
Pairs or small groups of teachers work collaboratively together to plan integrated units of work. As a result, purposeful professional dialogue takes place with teachers thinking about teaching and learning.

OPPORTUNITIES FOR TALKING AND SHARING PRACTICAL IDEAS

Regular and systematic opportunities for talk about integrated curriculum approaches are necessary. Activities such as 'tactic workshops' and 'this works for me' allow teachers to engage in practical, purposeful and classroom-focused sharing and discussion. These opportunities to talk help build a shared language and thus prevent many misunderstandings.

WATCHING EACH OTHER TEACH

Carefully negotiated and voluntary observation in classrooms is a powerful way of supporting teacher learning about the logistics of implementation. It is preferable that such observation of teaching is followed by reflection, analysis and feedback in a nonpersonal and practical manner.

PROBLEM SOLVING TOGETHER

This involves action research on shared problems associated with the classroom change. Feasible solutions to the teacher identified problems are developed and tested, then shared with others.

STAGE 3: CONTINUATION OF IMPLEMENTATION

Sustaining an integrated approach to curriculum design and practice

At this stage, care is taken to reaffirm what was learned from the initial implementation and to refine and adapt classroom practice as necessary. This is when teachers who have been reluctant to implement the change in their classrooms may be available to consider the first steps towards an integrated approach if appropriate strategies are used. Teachers who have been involved in the early implementation and have experienced success, now start to fine-tune their practice and show real commitment, confidence, knowledge and skill.

Guidelines to support the change process at stage 3 include:

1 Consider and take action on information from evaluation of initial implementation

Evaluation processes should be established during the initial implementation of an integrated curriculum approach. Such evaluation involves gathering information; arranging, organising and displaying this information in such a way that it can inform stakeholders about the needs, intentions, implementation processes and outcomes; and doing this with the ultimate purpose of helping quality decision making about student learning, teaching and structures.

School-level evaluation is a process which the school community initiates, conducts and uses for purposes which include:

- building the confidence and trust of stakeholders (the purpose of accountability)
- ensuring higher-level understanding of what is happening in the school (purpose of enlightenment)
- moving the school to a preferred/improved situation (the purpose of improvement),

Program evaluation needs to be more systematic and more explicit than everyday informal judgements. It is part of whole school planning; it is a crucial element of program planning/budgeting and should become part of the regular routine of the school. Each year the curriculum programs of the school should be subjected to either a major or minor evaluation — the difference in the two being in terms of scale and complexity. In this case a minor evaluation would be sufficient to provide guidance for continuation of the program.

2 Acknowledge that curriculum change is often associated with change in attitudes towards teaching and learning

A curriculum change of this nature may threaten teachers because it can invalidate the accumulated wisdom derived from their previous experience. Classroom practice and attitudes to teaching and learning can be challenged by a move to integrated curriculum.

Changes in attitudes or beliefs about new approaches to teaching and learning usually follow rather than precede changes in teaching practice. If teachers are supported while they experience something new for themselves, and it can be seen to work with students, then they are more likely to be prepared to modify their attitudes.

Thus, professional development should aim primarily at changing the teachers' environment so that new classroom practice is more attractive to them. Attitudes are more likely to change if teachers can be convinced to undertake small changes in their practice.

3 Remember that teachers will be at different stages of concern and implementation of the change

Research conducted at the University of Texas by Hall and his colleagues (1980) supports the assertion that individual teachers move through the curriculum implementation process in different ways and at different rates. They argue that at least two teacher dimensions need examination, an affective dimension (stages of concern) and a behavioural dimension (levels of use). Some teachers, when faced with a proposal for curriculum change, exhibit personal concerns, some exhibit task concerns, and some show concerns about the impact of the change on others, including the students. Similarly, teachers exhibit different sophistication in the use of curriculum. Some teachers are satisfied with routine use of the curriculum in a passive manner way, others insist on refining, extending, and challenging the ideas and practices of the curriculum.

Professional development actions at this stage of the change process should include:

Planned review of initial implementation

Systematic evaluation during the initial implementation stage is essential if classroom practice is to be sustained. A minor evaluation of the implementation to this stage should be undertaken by all staff involved in the program. Information should be collected on aspects such as:

- strengths of the program, things that should not be changed
- information needs, things that should be investigated
- things that, if worked on, will further improve the program
- resource needs to make improvement possible.

Using the information collected in the evaluation, teachers already involved in the program must have the opportunity to plan further action. Such plans should have the potential to improve the program.

Support for teachers ready for initial implementation

It is to be expected that individual teachers differ in their availability for learning, and that they implement change in differnt ways and at different rates. Change strategies should acknowledge these differences and vary accordingly. It follows that some teachers will only become available to consider a change to an integrated approach to curriculum design and practice after they have had the opportunity to observe it in practice for some time. Other teachers will still be unavailable. Teachers ready for the first small steps must be supported in the ways outlined in stage 2.

REFERENCES

Adams, D. 1990. *Children and science,* unpublished article, The University of Melbourne.

Brown, H. & Mathie, V. 1990, *Inside Whole Language: A Classroom View,* Heinemann Ed., Portsmouth.

Boomer, G. 1992, *Negotiating the Curriculum,* Taylor and Francis, New York.

Cambourne, B. 1988, *The Whole Story,* Ashton Scholastic, Gosford.

Clark, D. 1988, in *MCTP Assesment Alternatives,* CDC, Canberra.

Doyle, W. & Ponder, G. 1977, 'The practicality ethic in teacher decision-making', *Interchange,* vol. 78.8 (3), pp. 1-22.

Fullan, M. and Steigelbauer, S. 1991, *The New Meaning of Education Change,* 2nd edn, Teacher's College Press, New York.

Fullan, M. and Hargreaves, A. 1991, *Working Together for Your School,* ACER Paperbacks, Melbourne.

Guskey, T.R. 1985, 'Staff development and teacher change', *Educational Leadership,* April, pp. 57-60.

Hall, G.E. 1980, 'Using the individual and the innovation as the frame of reference for research on change', *Australian Educational Researcher,* vol. 7. no. 2, pp. 5-32.

Halliday, M. 1982, 'Three aspects of children's language development: Learning language, learning through language, learning about language', in *Oral and Written Language Research: Impact on the Schools,* eds. Y. Goodman, M. Haussler, and D. Strickland, NCTE, Urbana.

Hornsby, D., Sukarna, D. & Parry, J. 1988, *Read On: A Conference Approach to Reading,* Heinemann Ed., Portsmouth.

Jagger, A. & Smith-Burke, M. (eds.) 1985, *Observing the Language Learner,* International Reading Association, Newark.

Ministry of Education, Victoria. 1986, *Extending Children's Special Abilities,* Melbourne.

Ministry of Education, Victoria. 1988a, *Learning Through an Intergrated Curriculum: Approaches and Guidelines,* Melbourne.

Ministry of Education, Victoria. 1988b, *School Curriculum and Organisation Framework,* Melbourne.

Newell, S. & Stubbs, B. 1990, 'Developing literacy for life', in *Literacy for Life*, D. & H. Dufty, Dellasta, Melbourne.

Novak, J. 1988, 'Learning science and the science of learning', *Studies in Science Education*, vol. 15, pp. 71-101.

Parry, J. & Hornsby, D. 1988, *Write On: A Conference Approach to Writing*, Heinemann Ed., Portsmouth.

Pigdon, K. & Woolley, M. (in press), *Resourcing Children's Learning*, Macmillan, Melbourne.

Roughsey, D. 1975, *The Rainbow Serpent*, Collins, Sydney.

Schon, D.A. 1987, *Educating the Reflective Practitioner*, Jossey-Bass, San Francisco.

Simpson, M. 1990, 'Involving the whole school and the community', in *Literacy for Life*, D. & .H. Dufty, Dellasta, Melbourne.

Stice, C. 1987, 'Hierarchial concept mapping in the early grades', *Childhood-Education*, vol. 64, pp. 86-96, December.

Stow, H. 1989, *Tell It on Video*, Martin Education, Sydney.

Wickert, R. 1989, *No Single Measure*, Institute for Technical and Adult Teacher Education, Sydney.

Wilson, J. & Egeberg, P. 1989, *Co-operative Challenges*, Nelson, Melbourne.

Index

A selection of titles from Eleanor Curtain Publishing

The Literacy Agenda: Issues for the nineties
Edited by Elaine Furniss and Pamela Green   ISBN 1 857327 088   illustrtaed 178pp

A book to provoke, encourage and inspire you to 'have a go' at confronting the key issues of literacy development in your own classroom:
- How children learn to read
- What happens if they don't succeed
- Equal opportunities for girls and boys
- How to use the literacy cultures that children bring to the classroom
- The sort of talk that takes palce in classrooms
- Assessment procedures
- Second language learners
- How to involve parents
    Each chapter is a collaboration between a leading teacher educator and a classroom teacher. The practical implications of each issue discussed are always addressed.

The Literacy Connection: Language and learning across the curriculum
Edited by Elaine Furniss and Pamela Green   ISBN 1 875327 09 6   illustrated 178pp

How can you encourage and support children as they acquire the particular language skills needed for each subject discipline? *The Literacy Connection* explores ways so important for them if they are to gain control over their world:
- Selecting fiction that encourages literacy growth through the imaginative use of language
- Making factual texts 'user friendly' for the young reader-writer
- Imparting a confident command of the language of schooling
- Understanding the conventions of the language of science
- Fostering literacy development through drama and mathematics
- Understanding the potential of computers in language development
    The Literacy Connection will demand on active response to the question: what does it mean for my teaching, right now? You will want to investigate these ideas further in your own classroom.

Reading with Writing Communities: Co-operative Literacy Learning in the Classroom
Susan Hill and Joelle Hancock   ISBN 1 875327 12 6   illustrated 128pp

Co-operative learning, a way to organise and structure classroom experience has immense potential for improving the ways children learn. The links between co-operation and communication form a powerful base for learning in all subject areas.

   This book presents guide-lines, case studies and practical activities for creating a powerful reading and writing community within the classroom:

- Achieving gains in performance and achievement, equity, self-esteem and in social skills through co-operation and learning together
- Literature and the wider community, literature in the classroom, creating communities of readers and writers
- Building cohesion: creating the classroom culture
- Co-operative learning and literacy: the difference between co-operative and traditional groups: teaching co-operative skills
- Setting and meeting goals in reading
- Setting and meeting goals in writing
- Feedback, evaluation and goal setting

For information on these and other titles contact
Eleanor Curtain Publishing
906 Malvern Road, Armadale 3143, Australia
Tel (03) 822 0344   Fax (03) 824 8851

Distributed in New Zealand by
Ashton Scholastic
165 Marua Road, Panmure, Auckland
Tel (09) 579 6089   Fax (09) 579 3860